Fodor's 98
Pocket
Washington,
D.C.

Reprinted from *Fodor's Washington, D.C. 98*

Fodor's Travel Publications, Inc.
New York • Toronto • London • Sydney • Auckland
www.fodors.com/

Fodor's Pocket Washington, D.C.

EDITORS: Anastasia Redmond Mills and Audra Epstein

Editorial Contributors: Rob Andrews, Holly Bass, Anna Borgman, David Brown, Michael Dolan, John F. Kelly, Deborah Papier, Betty Ross, Heidi Sarna, Helayne Schiff, Dinah Spritzer, M. T. Schwartzman (Gold Guide editor), Dinah A. Spritzer, Bruce Walker, Jan Ziegler

Editorial Production: Stacey Kulig

Maps: David Lindroth, *cartographer*; Robert Blake, *map editor*

Design: Fabrizio La Rocca, *creative director*; Lyndell Brookhouse-Gil, *cover design*; Jolie Novak, *photo editor*

Production/Manufacturing: Mike Costa

Cover Photograph: James Lemass

Copyright

Special Sales

Fodor's Travel Publications are available at special discounts for bulk purchases for sales promotions or premiums. Special editions, including personalized covers, excerpts of existing guides, and corporate imprints, can be created in large quantities for special needs. For more information, contact your local bookseller or write to Special Markets, Fodor's Travel Publications, 201 East 50th Street, New York, NY 10022. Inquiries from Canada should be directed to your local Canadian bookseller or sent to Random House of Canada, Ltd., Marketing Department, 1265 Aerowood Drive, Mississauga, Ontario L4W 1B9. Inquiries from the United Kingdom should be sent to Fodor's Travel Publications, 20 Vauxhall Bridge Road, London SW1V 2SA.

PRINTED IN THE UNITED STATES OF AMERICA

10 9 8 7 6 5 4 3 2 1

CONTENTS

Maps

ON THE ROAD WITH FODOR'S

WE'RE ALWAYS thrilled to get letters from readers, especially one like this:

It took us an hour to decide what book to buy and we now know we picked the best one. Your book was wonderful, easy to follow, very accurate, and good on pointing out eating places, informal as well as formal. When we saw other people using your book, we would look at each other and smile.

Our editors and writers are deeply committed to making every Fodor's guide "the best one"— not only accurate but always charming, brimming with sound recommendations and solid ideas, right on the mark in describing restaurants and hotels, and full of fascinating facts that make you view what you've traveled to see in a rich new light.

New This Year

We're proud to announce that the American Society of Travel Agents has endorsed Fodor's as its guidebook of choice. ASTA is the world's largest and most influential travel trade association, operating in more than 170 countries, with 27,000 members pledged to adhere to a strict code of ethics reflecting the Society's motto, "Integrity in Travel." ASTA shares Fodor's devotion to providing smart, honest travel information and advice to travelers, and we've long recommended that our readers consult ASTA member agents for the experience and professionalism they bring to the table.

On the web, check out Fodor's site (www.fodors.com/), for information on major destinations around the world and travel-savvy interactive features. The Web site also lists the 85-plus stations nationwide that carry the *Fodor's Travel Show,* a live, call-in program that airs every weekend. Tune in to hear guests discuss their wonderful adventures—or call in to get answers for your most pressing travel questions.

How to Use This Book

Organization

Up front is **Essential Information.** Under each listing you'll find tips and information that will help you accomplish what you need to in Washington, D.C. You'll also find addresses and telephone numbers of organizations and companies that offer destination-related services and detailed information and publications.

The first chapter in the guide, Destination: Washington, D.C., helps get you in the mood for your trip. The Exploring chapter is subdivided by neighborhood; each subsection recommends neighborhood sights and lists them alphabetically. The remaining chapters are arranged in alphabetical order by subject (dining, lodging, nightlife and the arts, and shopping).

Icons and Symbols

★   Our special recommendations

✕   Restaurant

🏠   Lodging establishment

🐤   Good for kids (rubber duckie)

☞   Sends you to another section of the guide for more information

✉   Address

☎   Telephone number

🕐   Opening and closing times

💰   Admission prices (those we give apply to adults; substantially reduced fees are almost always available for children, students, and senior citizens)

Hotel Facilities

We always list the facilities that are available—but we don't specify whether they cost extra: When pricing accommodations, always ask what's included.

Assume that hotels operate on the **European Plan** (EP, with no meals) unless we note that they use the **Full American Plan** (FAP, with all meals), the **Modified American Plan** (MAP, with breakfast and dinner daily), or the **Continental Plan** (CP, with a Continental breakfast daily).

Restaurant Reservations and Dress Codes

Reservations are always a good idea; we note only when they're essential or when they are not accepted. Book as far ahead as you can, and reconfirm when you get to town. Unless otherwise noted, the restaurants listed are open daily for lunch and dinner. We mention dress only when men are required to wear a jacket or a jacket and tie.

Credit Cards

The following abbreviations are used: **AE**, American Express; **D**, Discover; **DC**, Diners Club; **MC**, MasterCard; and **V**, Visa.

Please Write to Us

You can use this book in the confidence that all prices and opening times are based on information supplied to us at press time; Fodor's cannot accept responsibility for any errors. Time inevitably brings changes, so always confirm information when it matters—especially if you're making a detour to visit a specific place. In addition, when making reservations be sure to mention if you have a disability or are traveling with children, if you prefer a private bath or a certain type of bed, or if you have specific dietary needs or any other concerns.

Were the restaurants we recommended as described? Did our hotel picks exceed your expectations? Did you find a museum we recommended a waste of time? If you have complaints, we'll look into them and revise our entries when the facts warrant it. If you've discovered a special place that we haven't included, we'll pass the information along to our correspondents and have them check it out. So send your feedback, positive *and* negative: E-mail us at editors@fodors.com (specifying the name of the editor on the subject line) or write to the Washington, D.C. editors at 201 East 50th Street, New York, NY 10022. Have a wonderful trip!

Karen Cure
Editorial Director

Washington, D.C. Area

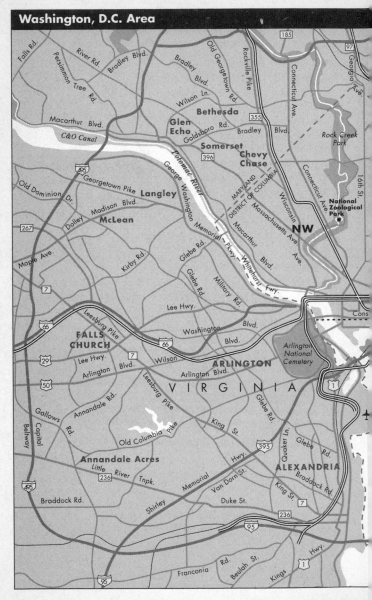

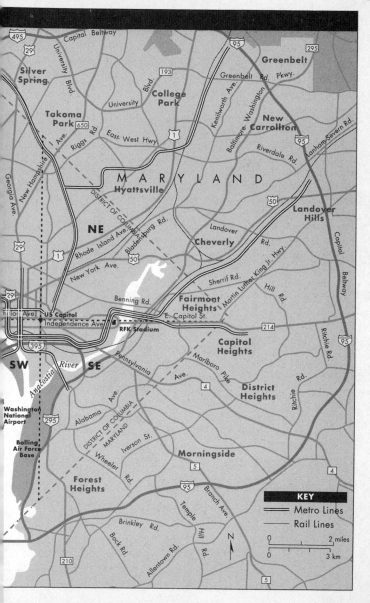

x

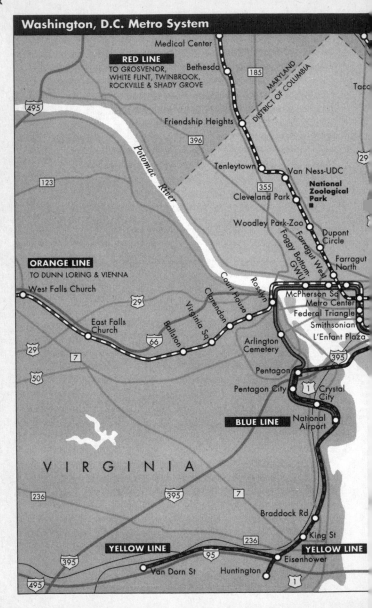

Washington, D.C. Metro System

RED LINE
TO GROSVENOR,
WHITE FLINT, TWINBROOK,
ROCKVILLE & SHADY GROVE

Medical Center
Bethesda
Friendship Heights
Tenleytown
Van Ness-UDC
National Zoological Park
Cleveland Park
Woodley Park-Zoo
Dupont Circle
Farragut North

ORANGE LINE
TO DUNN LORING & VIENNA
West Falls Church
East Falls Church
Ballston
Virginia Sq
Clarendon
Court House
Rosslyn
Foggy Bottom GWU
Farragut West
McPherson Sq
Metro Center
Federal Triangle
Smithsonian
L'Enfant Plaza
Arlington Cemetery
Pentagon
Pentagon City
Crystal City
BLUE LINE
National Airport

V I R G I N I A

Braddock Rd
King St
YELLOW LINE
Eisenhower
YELLOW LINE
Van Dorn St
Huntington

Potomac River

MARYLAND
DISTRICT OF COLUMBIA

Taco

185
495
396
123
355
29
29
66
7
50
236
395
7
236
95
395
495
1
1
395

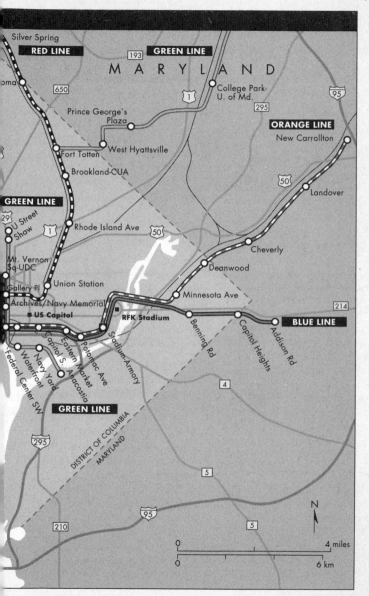

RED LINE   193   GREEN LINE

M A R Y L A N D

650   College Park-
U. of Md.   95

oma

Prince George's
Plaza   295

ORANGE LINE

Fort Totten   West Hyattsville   New Carrollton

Brookland-CUA   50   Landover

GREEN LINE

29   U Street
Shaw   1   Rhode Island Ave   50   Cheverly

Mt. Vernon
Sq-UDC   Deanwood

Gallery Pl   Union Station

Archives/Navy Memorial   Minnesota Ave

US Capitol   RFK Stadium   214

Eastern Market   BLUE LINE

Capitol S.   Anacostia   Benning Rd   Capitol Heights   Addison Rd

Navy Yard   Potomac Ave

Federal Center SW   Stadium-Armory

Waterfront

295   GREEN LINE

4

DISTRICT OF COLUMBIA
MARYLAND

210   95   5   5

N

0   4 miles

0   6 km

ESSENTIAL INFORMATION

Basic Information on Traveling in Washington, D.C., Savvy Tips to Make Your Trip a Breeze, and Companies and Organizations to Contact

AIR TRAVEL

MAJOR AIRLINE OR LOW-COST CARRIER?

Most people choose a flight based on price. Yet there are other issues to consider. Major airlines offer the greatest number of departures; smaller airlines—including regional, low-cost, and no-frill airlines—usually have a more limited number of flights daily. Major airlines have frequent-flyer partners, which allow you to credit mileage earned on one airline to your account with another. Low-cost airlines offer a definite price advantage and fewer restrictions, such as advance-purchase requirements. Safety-wise, low-cost carriers as a group have a good history, but **check the safety record before booking** any low-cost carrier; call the Federal Aviation Administration's Consumer Hotline (☞ Airline Complaints, *below*).

➤ MAJOR AIRLINES: **Air Canada** (☎ 800/776–3000) to National, Dulles, BWI. **America West** (☎ 800/235–9292) to National, Dulles, BWI. **American** (☎ 800/433–7300) to National, Dulles, BWI. **Continental** (☎ 800/525–0280) to National, Dulles, BWI.

Delta (☎ 800/221–1212) to National, Dulles, BWI. **Northwest** (☎ 800/225–2525) to National, Dulles, BWI. **TWA** (☎ 800/221–2000) to National, Dulles, BWI. **United** (☎ 800/241–6522) to National, Dulles, BWI. **US Airways** (☎ 800/428–4322) to National, Dulles, BWI.

➤ SMALLER AIRLINES: **Midway** (☎ 800/446–4392) to National. **Midwest Express** (☎ 800/452–2022) to National. **Southwest** (☎ 800/435–9792) to BWI. **Western Pacific** (☎ 800/930–3030) to Dulles.

➤ FROM THE U.K.: **British Airways** (☎ 0345/222111). **United** (☎ 0800/888555). **Virgin Atlantic** (☎ 01293/747747).

GET THE LOWEST FARE

The least-expensive airfares to Washington, D.C., are priced for round-trip travel. Major airlines usually require that you **book in advance and buy the ticket within 24 hours,** and you may have to **stay over a Saturday night.** It's smart to **call a number of airlines, and when you are quoted a good price, book it on the spot**—the same fare may not be available on the same flight the next day. Airlines generally allow you to change your return date for a fee $25–$50. If you don't use your ticket you can apply the cost toward the purchase of a new ticket, again for a small charge. However, most low-fare tickets are nonrefundable. To get the lowest airfare, **check different routings.** If your destination or home city has more than one gateway, compare prices to and from different airports. Also price off-peak flights, which may be significantly less expensive.

To save money on flights from the United Kingdom and back, **look into an APEX or Super-PEX ticket.** APEX tickets must be booked in advance and have certain restrictions. Super-PEX tickets can be purchased at the airport on the day of departure—subject to availability.

DON'T STOP UNLESS YOU MUST

When you book, **look for nonstop flights** and **remember that "direct" flights stop at least once.** Try to **avoid connecting flights,** which require a change of plane. Two airlines may jointly operate a connecting flight, so ask if your airline operates every segment—you may find that your preferred carrier flies you only part of the way.

USE AN AGENT

Travel agents, especially those who specialize in finding the lowest fares can be especially helpful when booking a plane ticket. When you're quoted a price, **ask your agent if the price is likely to get any lower.** Good agents know the seasonal fluctuations of airfares and can usually anticipate a sale or fare war. However, waiting can be risky: The fare could go *up* as seats become scarce, and you may wait so long that your preferred flight sells out. A wait-and-see strategy works best if your plans are flexible, but if you must arrive and depart on certain dates, don't delay.

AVOID GETTING BUMPED

Airlines routinely overbook planes, knowing that not everyone with a ticket will show up, but sometimes everyone does. When that happens, airlines ask for volunteers to give up their seats. In return these volunteers usually get a certificate for a free flight and are rebooked on the next flight out. If there are not enough volunteers the airline must choose who will be denied boarding. The first to get bumped are passengers who checked in late and those flying on discounted tickets, **so get to the gate and check in as early as possible,** especially during peak periods.

Always **bring a photo ID to the airport.** You may be asked to show it before you are allowed to check in.

ENJOY THE FLIGHT

For better service, **fly smaller or regional carriers,** which often have higher passenger-satisfaction ratings. Sometimes you'll find leather seats, more legroom, and better food. For more legroom, **request an emergency-aisle seat**; don't, however, sit in the row in front of the emergency aisle or in front of a bulkhead, where seats may not recline. If you don't like airline food, **ask for special meals when booking.** These can be vegetarian, low-cholesterol, or kosher, for example.

COMPLAIN IF NECESSARY

If your baggage goes astray or your flight goes awry, complain right away. Most carriers require that you file a claim immediately.

➤ AIRLINE COMPLAINTS: U.S. Department of Transportation **Aviation Consumer Protection Division** (⊠ C-75, Room 4107, Washington, DC 20590, ☎ 202/366–2220). **Federal Aviation Administration (FAA) Consumer Hotline** (☎ 800/322–7873).

AIRPORTS & TRANSFERS

The major gateways to Washington, D.C. include **National Airport,** in Virginia, 4 miles south of downtown Washington; **Dulles International Airport,** 26 miles west of Washington; and **Baltimore-Washington International (BWI) Airport,** in Maryland, about 25 miles northeast of Washington.

➤ AIRPORT INFORMATION: **National Airport** (☎ 703/417–8000). **Dulles International Airport** (☎ 703/661–2700). **Baltimore-Washington International (BWI) Airport** (☎ 410/859–7100).

TRANSFERS

➤ DULLES INTERNATIONAL AIRPORT: Taxis charge $45 for trips downtown.

Washington Flyer (☎ 703/685–1400) buses will take you to 1517 K Street NW, where you can board a free shuttle bus that serves downtown hotels. The ride from Dulles to downtown takes 45 minutes and costs $16 ($26 round-trip). The shuttle bus will also transport you from your hotel to the K Street address to catch the main airport bus on your return journey. Washington Flyer also provides service to Maryland and Virginia suburbs. Fares may be paid in cash or with Visa or MasterCard; children under age six ride free.

Call at least a day ahead and **Diplomat Limousine** (☎ 703/461–6800) will have a limousine waiting for you at the airport. The ride downtown costs $86.25, including tip. Call **Private Car** ahead of time to have a car waiting for you. The trip downtown costs $73.

➤ NATIONAL AIRPORT: Taxis charge about $13 to get from National Airport to downtown.

SuperShuttle buses (☎ 800/258–3826) depart for 1517 K Street NW every half hour. The 20-minute ride from National costs $8 ($14 round-trip). Drivers accept traveler's checks and major credit cards in addition to cash.

Call at least a day ahead and **Diplomat Limousine** (☎ 703/461–6800) will have a limousine waiting for you at the airport. The ride downtown costs $86.25, including tip. Call **Private Car** ahead of time to have a car waiting for you. The trip downtown costs $45.

If you are coming into National Airport, have little to carry, and are staying at a hotel near a subway stop, it makes sense to take the Metro downtown. The station is within walking distance of the baggage claim area, but a free airport shuttle stops outside each terminal and brings you to the National Airport station. The Metro ride downtown takes about 20 minutes and costs either $1.10 or $1.40, depending on the time of day.

➤ BALTIMORE-WASHINGTON INTERNATIONAL (BWI) AIRPORT: Taxis charge $50 for trips downtown.

SuperShuttle buses (☎ 800/258–3826) depart for 1517 K Street NW every hour. The 65-minute ride from BWI costs $21 ($31 round-trip). Drivers accept traveler's checks and major credit cards in addition to cash.

Call at least a day ahead and **Diplomat Limousine** (☎ 703/461–6800) will have a limousine waiting for you at the airport. The ride downtown costs $86.25, including tip.

Private Car (☎ 800/685–0888) has a counter at BWI Airport and charges $63 from there to downtown.

BUS TRAVEL

Washington is a major terminal for **Greyhound Bus Lines.** The company also has stations in nearby Silver Spring and Laurel, Maryland, and in Arlington and Springfield, Virginia. Check with your local Greyhound ticket office for prices and schedules.

WMATA's red, white, and blue Metrobuses crisscross the city and nearby suburbs, with some routes running 24 hours a day. All bus rides within the District are $1.10. Free transfers, good for 1½ to 2 hours, are available on buses and in Metro stations. Bus-to-bus transfers are accepted at designated Metrobus transfer points. Rail-to-bus transfers must be picked up before boarding the train. There may be a transfer charge when boarding the bus. There are no bus-to-rail transfers.

➤ INFORMATION: **Greyhound Bus Lines** (✉ 1005 1st St. NE, ☎ 202/289–5160 or 800/231–2222). **Washington Metropolitan Area Transit Authority** (WMATA, ☎ 202/637–7000, TTY 202/

638–3780; open weekdays 6 AM–10:30 PM and weekends 8 AM–10:30 PM) for schedule and route information.

CAR RENTAL

Rates in Washington D.C. begin at $38 a day and $139 a week for an economy car with air-conditioning, automatic transmission, and unlimited mileage. This does not include tax on car rentals, which is 8%.

➤ MAJOR AGENCIES: **Alamo** (☎ 800/327–9633, 0800/272–2000 in the U.K.). **Avis** (☎ 800/331–1212, 800/879–2847 in Canada). **Budget** (☎ 800/527–0700, 0800/181181 in the U.K.). **Dollar** (☎ 800/800–4000; 0990/565656 in the U.K., where it is known as Eurodollar). **Hertz** (☎ 800/654–3131, 800/263–0600 in Canada, 0345/555888 in the U.K.). **National InterRent** (☎ 800/227–7368; 0345/222525 in the U.K., where it is known as Europcar InterRent).

CUT COSTS

To get the best deal, **book through a travel agent who is willing to shop around.** When pricing cars, **ask about the location of the rental lot.** Some off-airport locations offer lower rates, and their lots are only minutes from the terminal via complimentary shuttle. You also may want to **price local car-rental companies,** whose rates may be lower still, although their

service and maintenance may not be as good as those of a name-brand agency. Remember to ask about required deposits, cancellation penalties, and drop-off charges if you're planning to pick up the car in one city and leave it in another.

Also **ask your travel agent about a company's customer-service record.** How has it responded to late plane arrivals and vehicle mishaps? Are there often lines at the rental counter, and, if you're traveling during a holiday period, does a confirmed reservation guarantee you a car?

Be sure to **look into wholesalers,** companies that do not own fleets but rent in bulk from those that do and often offer better rates than traditional car-rental operations. Prices are best during off-peak periods.

➤ RENTAL WHOLESALERS: The **Kemwel Group** (☎ 914/835–5555 or 800/678–0678, FAX 914/835–5126).

NEED INSURANCE?

When driving a rented car you are generally responsible for any damage to or loss of the vehicle. You also are liable for any property damage or personal injury that you may cause while driving. Before you rent, **see what coverage you already have** under the terms of your personal auto-insurance policy and credit cards.

For about $14 a day, rental companies sell protection, known as a collision- or loss-damage waiver (CDW or LDW) that eliminates your liability for damage to the car; it's always optional and should never be automatically added to your bill.

In most states you don't need CDW if you have personal auto insurance or other liability insurance. However, **make sure you have enough coverage to pay for the car.** If you do not have auto insurance or an umbrella policy that covers damage to third parties, purchasing CDW or LDW is highly recommended.

BEWARE SURCHARGES

Before you pick up a car in one city and leave it in another, **ask about drop-off charges or one-way service fees,** which can be substantial. Note, too, that some rental agencies charge extra if you return the car before the time specified on your contract. To avoid a hefty refueling fee, **fill the tank just before you turn in the car,** but be aware that gas stations near the rental outlet may overcharge.

MEET THE REQUIREMENTS

In the United States you must be 21 to rent a car, and rates may be higher if you're under 25. Residents of the U.K. will need a reservation voucher, a passport, a U.K. driver's license, and a travel policy that covers each driver, in order to pick up a car.

CUSTOMS & DUTIES

ENTERING THE U.S.

Visitors age 21 and over may import the following into the United States: 200 cigarettes or 50 cigars or 2 kilograms of tobacco, 1 liter of alcohol, and gifts worth $100. Prohibited items include meat products, seeds, plants, and fruits.

ENTERING CANADA

If you've been out of Canada for at least seven days you may bring in C$500 worth of goods duty-free. If you've been away for fewer than seven days but more than 48 hours, the duty-free allowance drops to C$200; if your trip lasts 24–48 hours, the allowance is C$50. You may not pool allowances with family members. Goods claimed under the C$500 exemption may follow you by mail; those claimed under the lesser exemptions must accompany you.

Alcohol and tobacco products may be included in the seven-day and 48-hour exemptions but not in the 24-hour exemption. If you meet the age requirements of the province or territory through which you reenter Canada you may bring in, duty-free, 1.14 liters (40 imperial ounces) of wine or liquor *or* 24 12-ounce cans or bottles of beer or ale. If you are 16 or older you may bring in, duty-free, 200 cigarettes and 50 cigars; these items must accompany you.

You may send an unlimited number of gifts worth up to C$60 each duty-free to Canada. Label the package UNSOLICITED GIFT—VALUE UNDER $60. Alcohol and tobacco are excluded.

➤ INFORMATION: **Revenue Canada** (✉ 2265 St. Laurent Blvd. S, Ottawa, Ontario K1G 4K3, ☎ 613/993–0534, 800/461–9999 in Canada).

ENTERING THE U.K.
From countries outside the EU, including the United States, you may import, duty-free, 200 cigarettes or 50 cigars; 1 liter of spirits or 2 liters of fortified or sparkling wine or liqueurs; 2 liters of still table wine; 60 milliliters of perfume; 250 milliliters of toilet water; plus £136 worth of other goods, including gifts and souvenirs.

➤ INFORMATION: **HM Customs and Excise** (✉ Dorset House, Stamford St., London SE1 9NG, ☎ 0171/202–4227).

INSURANCE

Travel insurance is the best way to **protect yourself against financial loss.** The most useful policies are trip-cancellation-and-interruption, default, medical, and comprehensive insurance.

Without insurance you will lose all or most of your money if you cancel your trip, regardless of the reason. It's essential that you **buy trip-cancellation-and-interruption insurance,** particularly if your airline ticket, cruise, or package tour is nonrefundable and cannot be changed. When considering how much coverage you need, look for a policy that will cover the cost of your trip plus the nondiscounted price of a one-way airline ticket, should you need to return home early. Also **consider default or bankruptcy insurance,** which protects you against a supplier's failure to deliver.

Citizens of the United Kingdom can buy an annual travel-insurance policy valid for most vacations during the year in which it's purchased. If you are pregnant or have a preexisting medical condition, make sure you're covered. According to the Association of British Insurers, a trade association representing 450 insurance companies, it's wise to buy extra medical coverage when you visit the United States.

Always **buy travel insurance directly from the insurance company;** if you buy it from a travel agency or tour operator that goes out of business you probably will not be covered for the agency or operator's default, a major risk. Before you make any purchase, **review your existing health and home-owner's policies** to find out whether they cover expenses incurred while traveling.

➤ U.S. TRAVEL INSURERS: **Access America** (✉ 6600 W. Broad St., Richmond, VA 23230, ☎ 804/

285–3300 or 800/284–8300),
Carefree Travel Insurance (⊠ Box
9366, 100 Garden City Plaza,
Garden City, NY 11530, ☎ 516/
294–0220 or 800/323–3149),
Near Travel Services (⊠ Box
1339, Calumet City, IL 60409,
☎ 708/868–6700 or 800/654–
6700), **Travel Guard International**
(⊠ 1145 Clark St., Stevens Point,
WI 54481, ☎ 715/345–0505 or
800/826–1300), **Travel Insured
International** (⊠ Box 280568,
East Hartford, CT 06128–0568,
☎ 860/528–7663 or 800/243–
3174), **Travelex Insurance Services**
(⊠ 11717 Burt St., Suite 202,
Omaha, NE 68154-1500, ☎ 402/
445–8637 or 800/228–9792,
FAX 800/867–9531), **Wallach &
Company** (⊠ 107 W. Federal St.,
Box 480, Middleburg, VA 20118,
☎ 540/687–3166 or 800/237–
6615). In Canada, **Mutual of
Omaha** (⊠ Travel Division, 500
University Ave., Toronto, Ontario
M5G 1V8, ☎ 416/598–4083,
800/268–8825 in Canada).

➤ U.K. TRAVEL INSURERS: **Association of British Insurers** (⊠ 51
Gresham St., London EC2V 7HQ,
☎ 0171/600–3333).

MONEY

ATMS
Before leaving home, **make sure
that your credit cards have been
programmed for ATM use.**

➤ ATM LOCATIONS: **Cirrus**
(☎ 800/424–7787). **Plus**
(☎ 800/843–7587).

PASSPORTS & VISAS

CANADIANS
Canadians do not need a passport
to enter the United States.

U.K. CITIZENS
British citizens need a valid passport to enter the United States. If
you are staying for fewer than 90
days, with a return or onward
ticket, you probably will not need
a visa. However, you will need to
fill out the Visa Waiver Form,
1-94W, supplied by the airline.

➤ INFORMATION: **London Passport
Office** (☎ 0990/21010) for fees
and documentation requirements
and to request an emergency pass-
port. **U.S. Embassy Visa Informa-
tion Line** (☎ 01891/200–290) for
U.S. visa information; calls cost
49p per minute. **U.S. Embassy
Visa Branch** (⊠ 5 Upper Gros-
venor St., London W1A 2JB) for
U.S. visa information; send a self-
addressed, stamped envelope.
Write the **U.S. Consulate General**
(⊠ Queen's House, Queen St.,
Belfast BTI 6EO) if you live in
Northern Ireland.

SUBWAY TRAVEL
The WMATA provides bus and
subway service in the District and
in the Maryland and Virginia suburbs. The Metro, opened in 1976,
is one of the country's cleanest
and safest subway systems. Trains
run weekdays 5:30 AM–midnight,
weekends 8 AM–midnight. During
the weekday rush hours (5:30–

9:30 AM and 3–8 PM), trains come along every six minutes. At other times and on weekends and holidays, trains run about every 12–15 minutes. The base fare is $1.10; the actual price you pay depends on the time of day and the distance traveled.

Buy your ticket at the Farecard machines; they accept coins and crisp $1, $5, $10, or $20 bills. The Farecard should be inserted into the turnstile to enter the platform. **Make sure you hang onto the card—you'll need it to exit at your destination.**

Some Washingtonians report that the Farecard's magnetic strip interferes with the strips on ATM cards and credit cards, so **keep the cards separated in your pocket or wallet.**

➤ INFORMATION: **Washington Metropolitan Area Transit Authority** (WMATA; ☎ 202/637–7000, TTY 202/638–3780; open weekdays 6 AM–10:30 PM, weekends 8 AM–10:30 PM).

TAXIS

Taxis in the District are not metered; they operate instead on a curious zone system. **Before you set off, ask your cab driver how much the fare will be.** The basic single rate for traveling within one zone is $3.20. There is an extra $1.25 charge for each additional passenger and a $1 surcharge during the 4–6:30 PM rush hour. Bulky suitcases are charged at a higher rate, and $1.50 is tacked on when you phone for a cab.

TELEPHONES

CALLING HOME
AT&T, MCI, and Sprint long-distance services make calling home relatively convenient and let you avoid hotel surcharges. Typically you dial an 800 number in the United States.

TOUR OPERATORS

Buying a prepackaged tour or independent vacation can make your trip to Washington, D.C., less expensive and more hassle-free. Because everything is prearranged you'll spend less time planning.

Operators that handle several hundred thousand travelers per year can use their purchasing power to give you a good price. Their high volume may also indicate financial stability. But some small companies provide more personalized service; because they tend to specialize, they may also be more knowledgeable about a given area.

A GOOD DEAL?
The more your package or tour includes, the better you can predict the cost of your vacation. Make sure you know exactly what is covered, and **beware of hidden costs.** Are taxes, tips, and service charges included? Transfers and baggage handling? Entertainment and excursions? These can add up.

If the package or tour you are considering is priced lower than in your wildest dreams, **be skeptical.** Also, **make sure your travel agent knows the accommodations** and other services.

BUYER BEWARE

Each year consumers are stranded or lose their money when tour operators—even very large ones with excellent reputations—go out of business. So **check out the operator.** Find out how long the company has been in business, and ask several agents about its reputation. **Don't book unless the firm has a consumer-protection program.**

Members of the National Tour Association and United States Tour Operators Association are required to set aside funds to cover your payments and travel arrangements in case the company defaults. Nonmembers may carry insurance instead. Look for the details, and for the name of an underwriter with a solid reputation, in the operator's brochure. Note: When it comes to tour operators, **don't trust escrow accounts.** Although the Department of Transportation watches over charter-flight operators, no regulatory body prevents tour operators from raiding the till. You may want to protect yourself by buying travel insurance that includes a tour-operator default provision. For more information, *see* Consumer Protection, *above.*

It's also a good idea to choose a company that participates in the American Society of Travel Agent's Tour Operator Program (TOP). This gives you a forum if there are any disputes between you and your tour operator; ASTA will act as mediator.

➤ TOUR-OPERATOR RECOMMENDATIONS: **National Tour Association** (✉ NTA, 546 E. Main St., Lexington, KY 40508, ☎ 606/226–4444 or 800/755–8687). **United States Tour Operators Association** (✉ USTOA, 342 Madison Ave., Suite 1522, New York, NY 10173, ☎ 212/599–6599, FAX 212/599–6744). **American Society of Travel Agents** (☞ *below*).

USING AN AGENT

Travel agents are excellent resources. In fact, large operators accept bookings made only through travel agents. But it's a good idea to **collect brochures from several agencies,** because some agents' suggestions may be influenced by relationships with tour and package firms that reward them for volume sales. If you have a special interest, **find an agent with expertise in that area;** ASTA (☞ Travel Agencies, *below*) has a database of specialists worldwide. Do some homework on your own, too: Local tourism boards can provide information about lesser-known and small-niche operators, some of which may sell only direct.

THEME TRIPS

➤ LEARNING: **Smithsonian Study Tours and Seminars** (✉ 1100 Jefferson Dr. SW, Room 3045, MRC 702, Washington, DC 20560, ☎ 202/357–4700, FAX 202/633–9250).

➤ PERFORMING ARTS: **Dailey-Thorp Travel** (✉ 330 W. 58th St., #610, New York, NY 10019–1817, ☎ 212/307–1555 or 800/998–4677, FAX 212/974–1420).

TRAIN TRAVEL

More than 80 trains a day arrive at Washington, D.C.'s **Union Station** on Capitol Hill (✉ 50 Massachusetts Ave. NE, ☎ 202/484–7540 or 800/872–7245).

TRAVEL AGENCIES

A good travel agent puts your needs first. Look for an agency that has been in business at least five years, emphasizes customer service, and has someone on staff who specializes in your destination. In addition, **make sure the agency belongs to the American Society of Travel Agents** (ASTA). If your travel agency is also acting as your tour operator, *see* Tour Operators *above*.

➤ LOCAL AGENT REFERRALS: **American Society of Travel Agents** (✉ ASTA, ☎ 800/965–2782 24-hr hot line, FAX 703/684–8319). **Alliance of Canadian Travel Associations** (✉ Suite 201, 1729 Bank St., Ottawa, Ontario K1V 7Z5, ☎ 613/521–0474, FAX 613/521–0805). **Association of British Travel Agents** (✉ 55–57 Newman St., London W1P 4AH, ☎ 0171/637–2444, FAX 0171/637–0713).

VISITOR INFORMATION

For general information, seasonal events, area B&Bs, and brochures, contact the city and state tourism offices below. For White House tours and special events call or visit the White House Visitor Center. For recorded messages about Park Service events and exhibits at the Smithsonian Institution museums, call the "Dial-a" numbers below. The National Parks Service has information kiosks around the city.

➤ CITYWIDE INFORMATION: **Washington, D.C. Convention and Visitors Association** (✉ 1212 New York Ave. NW, Suite 600, Washington, DC 20005, ☎ 202/789–7000, FAX 202/789–7037). **D.C. Committee to Promote Washington** (✉ 1212 New York Ave. NW, Suite 200, Washington, DC 20005, ☎ 202/724–5644 or 800/422–8644).

➤ EVENTS AND ATTRACTIONS: **White House Visitor Center** (✉ Baldrige Hall, Dept. of Commerce, 1450 Pennsylvania Ave. NW, ☎ 202/208–1631). **Dial-A-Park** (☎ 202/619–7275). **Dial-A-Museum** (☎ 202/357–2020).

➤ NATIONAL PARKS: **National Park Service** (✉ Office of Public Affairs, National Capital Region, 1100 Ohio Dr. SW, Washington, DC 20242, ☎ 202/619–7222, FAX 202/619–7302).

➤ STATEWIDE INFORMATION: **State of Maryland** (✉ Office of Tourist Development, 217 E. Redwood St., 9th floor, Baltimore, MD 21202, ☎ 410/767–3400, FAX 410/333–6643). **Virginia Tourism Corporation, Head Quarters:** (✉ 901 East Byrd St., Richmond, VA 23219, ☎ 804/786–4484, FAX 804/786–1919); Walk-In Office: (✉ 1629 K St. NW, Washington, D.C., 20006, ☎ 202/659–5523, FAX 202/659–8646; ☎ 800/934–9184) for accommodations at Virginia B&Bs.

➤ IN THE U.K.: **Washington D.C. Convention and Visitors Association** (✉ 375 Upper Richmond Rd. West, East Sheen, London SW14 7NX, ☎ 0181/392–9187, FAX 0181/392–1318). Brochures and maps can be obtained by enclosing a cheque, postal order or stamps to the value of £1.50.

WHEN TO GO

Washington has two delightful seasons: spring and autumn. In spring, the city's ornamental fruit trees are budding, and its many gardens are in bloom. By autumn, most of the summer crowds have left and visitors can enjoy the museums, galleries, and monuments in peace. Summers can be uncomfortably hot and humid (local legend has it that Washington was considered a "tropical hardship post" by some European diplomats). Winter witnesses the lighting of the National Christmas Tree and countless historic-house tours, but the weather is often bitter, with a handful of modest snowstorms that somehow bring this Southern city to a standstill. If you're interested in government, visit when Congress is in session. When lawmakers break for recess (at Christmas, Easter, July 4, and other holiday periods), the city seems a little less vibrant.

CLIMATE

What follows are the average daily maximum and minimum temperatures for Washington.

Jan.	47F	8C	May	76F	24C	Sept.	79F	26C
	34	– 1		58	14		61	16
Feb.	47F	8C	June	85F	29C	Oct.	70F	21C
	31	– 1		65	18		52	11
Mar.	56F	13C	July	88F	31C	Nov.	56F	13C
	38	3		70	21		41	5
Apr.	67F	19C	Aug.	86F	30C	Dec.	47F	8C
	47	8		68	20		32	0

➤ FORECASTS: **Weather Channel Connection** (☎ 900/932–8437), 95¢ per minute from a Touch-Tone phone.

1 Destination: Washington, D.C.

AMERICA'S HOMETOWN

TO A SURPRISING DEGREE, life in Washington is not that different from life elsewhere in the country. People are born here, grow up here, get jobs here—by no means invariably with the federal government—and go on to have children, who repeat the cycle. Very often, they live out their lives without ever testifying before Congress, being indicted for influence peddling, or attending a state dinner at the White House.

Which is not to say that the federal government does not cast a long shadow over the city. Among Washington's 543,000 inhabitants are an awful lot of lawyers, journalists, and people who include the word "policy" in their job titles. It's just that D.C. is much more of a hometown than most tourists realize.

Just a few blocks away from the monuments and museums on the Mall are residential and business districts whose scale is very human. The houses are a crazy quilt of architectural styles, kept in linear formation by rows of lush trees. On the commercial streets, bookstores and ethnic groceries abound.

Redevelopment has left its mark. Fourteenth Street was once the capital's red-light district. The city was determined to clean up the strip, and to everyone's surprise it succeeded. Nor is much left of the tacky commercial district around Ninth and F streets. Washington's original downtown, it deteriorated when the city's center shifted to the west, to the "new" downtown of Connecticut Avenue and K Street. But the "old" downtown is being rejuvenated. The department stores that once drew crowds with their window displays have been renovated; there are new hotels and office buildings; and as the construction dust clears, the area is looking pretty good.

Many people who come here are worried about crime. Crime is certainly a major problem, as it is in other big cities, but Washington is not nearly as dangerous as its well-publicized homicide rate might lead you to believe. Most visitors have relatively little to fear. The drug-related shootings that have in the past made Washington a murder capital generally take place in remote sections of the city. Unless you go seeking out the drug markets, there isn't much chance you'll get caught in the cross fire of rival drug gangs. Crimes against property are more widespread, but still far from ubiquitous. Unlike New York, Washington is not full of expert pickpockets; nor is it plagued by gold-chain snatchers.

The city's Metro is generally safe, even at night. However, if you have to walk from your stop in a neighborhood that isn't well lit and trafficked, you probably should invest in a taxi. Of course, even exercising normal prudence, it is still possible that you will have an encounter with someone who believes that what's yours ought to be his. If that happens, don't argue.

Your attachment to the contents of your wallet is certain to be tested in another way, however. Panhandlers are now a fixture of the cityscape, and there is no avoiding their importunities. How you respond to them is a matter only your conscience can advise you on. Wealth and poverty have always coexisted in America's hometown; but poverty is now omnipresent, wearing a very human face.

—Deborah Papier

A native of Washington, Deborah Papier has worked as an editor and writer for numerous newspapers and magazines.

2 Exploring Washington

By John F.
Kelly

Updated
by Bruce
Walker

TIRED OF ITS NOMADIC EXISTENCE after having set up shop in eight different locations, Congress voted in 1785 to establish a permanent "Federal town." Northern lawmakers wanted the capital on the Delaware River, in the north, southerners wanted it on the Potomac, in the south. A deal was struck when Virginia's Thomas Jefferson agreed to support the proposal that the federal government assume the war debts of the colonies if New York's Alexander Hamilton and other northern legislators would agree to locate the capital on the banks of the Potomac. George Washington himself selected the exact site of the capital, a diamond-shape, 100-square-mi plot that encompassed the confluence of the Potomac and Anacostia rivers, not far from the president's estate at Mount Vernon. To give the young city a bit of a head start, Washington included the already thriving tobacco ports of Alexandria, Virginia, and Georgetown, Maryland, in the District of Columbia.

Pierre-Charles L'Enfant, a young French engineer who had fought in the Revolution, offered his services in creating a capital "magnificent enough to grace a great nation." He wrote that his plan would "leave room for that aggrandizement and embellishment which the increase in the wealth of the nation will permit it to pursue at any period, however remote." At times it must have seemed remote indeed, for the town grew so slowly that when Charles Dickens visited Washington in 1842 what he saw were "spacious avenues that begin in nothing and lead nowhere; streets a mile long that only want houses, roads, and inhabitants; public buildings that need but a public to be complete and ornaments of great thoroughfares which need only great thoroughfares to ornament."

It took the Civil War—and every war thereafter—to energize the city, by attracting thousands of new residents and spurring building booms that extended the capital in all directions. Streets were paved in the 1870s and the first streetcars ran in the 1880s. Despite the growth and despite the fact that blacks have always played an important role in the city's history (black mathematician Benjamin Ban-

Exploring Washington, D.C. *(Boxes Refer to Detail Maps)*

Georgetown

Dupont Circle and Foggy Bottom

The White House Area

California St.

S St.

Decatur Pl.
R St.

Sheridan Circle

Florida Ave.

S St.

New Hampshire Ave.

R St.

Corcoran St.

Q St.

16th St.

15th St.

14th St.

R St.

Massachusetts Ave.

Q St.

22nd St.

21st St.

20th St.

Dupont Circle

Church St.

Q St.

17th St.

Church St.

Lo
C

19th St.

18th St.

P St.

O St.

Rhode Island Ave.

Q St.

P St.

O St.

N St.

Rock Creek

30th St.

29th St.

28th St.

27th St.

N St.

N St.

Connecticut Ave.

Scott Circle

15th St.

M St.

M St.

New Hampshire Ave.

M St.

16th St.

Thomas Circle

L St.

Washington Circle

L St.

K St.

25th St.

M St.

29

M St.

29

Pennsylvania Ave.

24th St.

23rd St.

22nd St.

H St.

New York

28th St.

G St.

F St.

The White House

15th St.

14th St.

Virginia Ave.

E St.

D St.

17th St.

C St.

Constitution Ave.

50

Washington Monument

Lincoln Memorial

Reflecting Pool

Arlington Memorial Br.

Independence Ave.

Kutz Br.

Ohio Dr.

West Potomac Park

W. Basin Dr.

Tidal Basin

Columbia Island

Outlet Br.

Potomac River

Ladybird Johnson Park

Jefferson Memorial

395

To Alexandria

The Monuments

NW ◆ NE

S St.

S St.

R St.

Florida Ave.

R St.

Q St.

Rhode Island Ave.

Q St.

P St.

O St.

O St.

N St.

New York Ave.

M St.

M St.

L St.

L St.

Mt. Vernon Square

Massachusetts

I St.

H St.

Old Downtown and Federal Triangle

Capitol Hill

G St.

F St.

E St.

Union Station

Columbus Memorial Fountain

Pennsylvania

Ave.

Stanton Park

D St.

Constitution Ave.

Louisiana Ave.

NE

Madison Dr.

National Gallery of Art

Smithsonian Institution

THE

MALL

National Air and Space Museum

US Capitol

E. Capitol St.

SE

Jefferson Dr.

Independence Ave.

Maryland Ave.

Folger Park

C St.

Canal St.

The Mall

D St.

Southwest Fwy.

New Jersey Ave.

E St.

G St.

Virginia Ave.

G St.

cis Case morial Br.

0   550 yards

0   500 meters

I St.

N

SW ◆ SE

Washington Canal

S St. R St. Q St. O St. N St. M St. L St. 9th St. 10th St. 11th St. 12th St. 8th St. 7th St. 6th St. 5th St. 4th St. 3rd St. 1st St. 2nd St. North Capitol St. Lincoln Rd. 3rd St. New Jersey Ave. Vermont Ave.

neker surveyed the land with Pierre L'Enfant in the 18th century), Washington today remains essentially segregated. Whites—who account for about 30% of the population— reside mostly in northwest Washington. Blacks live largely east of Rock Creek Park and south of the Anacostia River.

Washington is a city of other unfortunate contrasts: Citizens of the capital of the free world couldn't vote in a presidential election until 1964, weren't granted limited home rule until 1974, and are represented in Congress by a single nonvoting delegate (though in 1990 residents elected two "shadow" senators, one of whom is political gadfly Jesse Jackson). Homeless people sleep on steam grates next to multimillion-dollar government buildings, and a flourishing drug trade has earned Washington the dubious distinction of murder capital of the United States. Though it's little consolation to those affected, most crime is restricted to neighborhoods far from the areas visited by tourists.

Still, there's no denying that Washington, the world's first planned capital city, is also one of its most beautiful. And though the federal government dominates the city psychologically as much as the Washington Monument dominates it physically, there are parts of the capital where you can leave politics behind. The sections that follow will take you through the monumental city, the governmental city, and the residential city. As you explore, look for evidence of L'Enfant's hand, still present despite growing pains and frequent deviations from his plan. His Washington was to be a city of vistas—pleasant views that would shift and change from block to block, a marriage of geometry and art. It remains this way today. Like its main industry, politics, Washington's design is a constantly changing kaleidoscope that invites contemplation from all angles.

The Mall

The Mall is the heart of nearly every visitor's trip to Washington. With nearly a dozen diverse museums ringing the expanse of green, it's the closest thing the capital has to a theme park (unless you count the federal government itself, which has uncharitably been called "Disneyland on the Potomac"). As at a theme park, you may have to stand in an occasional line, but unlike the amusements at Disneyland almost everything you'll see here is free. (You may, however, need free, timed-entry tickets to some of the more popular traveling exhibitions. These are usually available at the museum information desk or by phone, for a service charge, from TicketMaster, at ☎ 202/432–7328.)

Of course, the Mall is more than just a front yard for all these museums. Bounded on the north and south by Constitution and Independence avenues, and on the east and west by 3rd and 14th streets, it's a picnicking park and a jogging path, an outdoor stage for festivals and fireworks, and America's town green. Nine of the Smithsonian Institution's fourteen museums in the capital lie within these boundaries. (The nearest Metro stops are Smithsonian, Archives/Navy Memorial, and L'Enfant Plaza).

Numbers in the margin correspond to points of interest on the Mall map.

Sights to See

⑫ **Arthur M. Sackler Gallery.** When Charles Freer endowed the gallery that bears his name (☞ Freer Gallery of Art, *below*), he insisted on a few conditions: objects in the collection could not be loaned out, nor could objects from outside the collections be put on display. Because of the latter restriction it was necessary to build a second, complementary museum to house the Asian art collection of Arthur M. Sackler, a wealthy medical researcher and publisher who allowed Smithsonian curators to select 1,000 items from his ample collection and pledged $4 million toward the construction of the museum. The collection includes works from China, the Indian subcontinent, Persia, Thailand, and Indonesia. Articles in the permanent collection include Chinese ritual bronzes, jade ornaments from the 3rd millennium BC, Persian manuscripts, and Indian paintings in gold, silver, lapis lazuli, and malachite. ⊠ *1050 Independence Ave. SW,* ☎ *202/357–2700, TTY 202/357–1729.* ☞ *Free.* ☉ *Daily 10–5:30. Metro: Smithsonian.*

❷ **Arts and Industries Building.** In 1876 Philadelphia hosted the United States International Exposition in honor of the nation's Centennial. After the festivities, scores of exhibitors donated American Victoriana to the federal government.

Arthur M.
Sackler
Gallery, **12**

Arts and
Industries
Building, **2**

Bureau of
Engraving and
Printing, **9**

Department of
Agriculture, **10**

Freer Gallery
of Art, **11**

Hirshhorn
Museum and
Sculpture
Garden, **3**

National Air
and Space
Museum, **4**

National
Gallery
of Art, **5**

National
Museum of
African Art, **13**

National
Museum of
American
History, **7**

National
Museum of
Natural
History, **6**

Smithsonian
Institution
Building, **1**

United States
Holocaust
Memorial
Museum, **8**

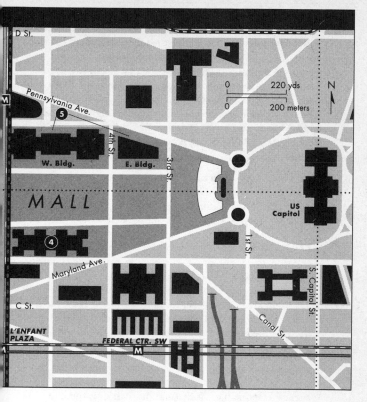

In order to house the objects that had suddenly come its way, the Smithsonian commissioned this redbrick and sandstone building, the second Smithsonian museum to be constructed. The building was originally called the United States National Museum, the name that is still engraved in stone above the doorway. Some of the objects on display—which include carriages, tools, furnishings, printing presses, even a steam locomotive—are from the original Philadelphia Centennial. ⊠ *900 Jefferson Dr. SW,* ☎ *202/357–2700, TTY 202/357–1729.* 🎟 *Free.* ☉ *Daily 10–5:30. Metro: Smithsonian.*

⑨ Bureau of Engraving and Printing. Paper money has been printed in this huge building since 1914, when they stopped printing it in the Auditor's Building. Despite the fact that there are no free samples, the self-guided tour of the bureau—which takes visitors past presses that turn out some $450 million a day—is one of the city's most popular. In addition to all the paper currency in the United States, stamps, military certificates, and presidential invitations are printed here too. ⊠ *14th and C Sts. SW,* ☎ *202/874–3019.* 🎟 *Free; Apr. 3–Sept. same-day timed-entry passes issued starting at 7:45 AM at Raoul Wallenberg Pl. SW entrance.* ☉ *Weekdays 9–2. Metro: Smithsonian.*

⑩ Department of Agriculture. Although there's nothing of interest to tourists inside, this sprawling complex is too gargantuan to ignore. The home of a major governmental agency responsible for setting and carrying out the nation's agricultural policies, it comprises two buildings. ⊠ *Independence Ave. between 12th and 14th Sts. SW. Metro: Smithsonian.*

⑪ Freer Gallery of Art. Housing one of the world's finest collections of masterpieces from Asia, the Smithsonian's Freer Gallery of Art was made possible by an endowment from Detroit industrialist Charles L. Freer, who retired in 1900 and devoted the rest of his life to collecting art. Opened in 1923, four years after its benefactor's death, its collection includes more than 26,000 works of art from the Far and Near East, including Asian porcelains, Japanese screens, Chinese paintings and bronzes, Korean stoneware, and examples of Islamic art. On display in Gallery 12 is the "Peacock Room," a blue-and-gold dining room decorated with painted leather, wood, and canvas. Freer paid $30,000 for the entire room and moved it from London to the United States in 1904. The works of American artists Freer felt were influenced by the Orient also are on display. ⊠ *12th St. and Jefferson Dr. SW,* ☎ *202/357–2700, TTY 202/357–1729.* ⊠ *Free.* ☉ *Daily 10–5:30. Metro: Smithsonian.*

❸ Hirshhorn Museum and Sculpture Garden. An architecturally striking but aesthetically controversial building that opened in 1974, the Hirshhorn manages a collection that includes 4,000 paintings and drawings and 2,000 sculptures donated by Joseph H. Hirshhorn, a Latvian-born immigrant who made his fortune in this country running uranium mines. American artists such as Eakins, Pollock, Rothko, and Stella are represented, as are modern European and Latin masters, including Francis Bacon, Fernando Botero, Magritte, Miró, and Victor Vasarely. The Hirshhorn's impressive sculpture collection is arranged in the open spaces between the museum's concrete piers and across Jefferson Drive in the sunken **Sculpture Garden.** The display in the Sculpture Garden includes one of the largest public American collections of works by Henry Moore (58 sculptures), as well as works by Honoré Daumier, Max Ernst, Alberto Giacometti, Pablo Picasso, and Man Ray. Auguste Rodin's *Burghers of Calais* is a highlight. ⊠ *Independence Ave. SW and 7th St.,* ☎ *202/357–2700, TTY 202/357–1729.* ⊠ *Free.* ☉ *Daily 10–5:30, sculpture garden open daily 7:30–dusk. Metro: Smithsonian.*

★ ☺ ❹ National Air and Space Museum. Opened in 1976, Air and Space is the most visited museum in the world, attracting more than eight million people each year. (It's thought to be the most-visited building on earth.) The 23 galleries tell the story of aviation from the earliest human attempts at flight. Suspended from the ceiling like plastic models in a child's room are dozens of aircraft, including the actual "Wright Flyer" that Wilbur Wright piloted over the sands of Kitty Hawk, North Carolina; Charles Lindbergh's "Spirit of St. Louis"; the X-1 rocket plane in which Chuck Yeager broke the sound barrier; and the X-15, the fastest plane ever built. Other highlights include a backup model of the Skylab orbital workshop that you can walk through; the

Voyager airplane that Dick Rutan and Jeana Yeager flew
nonstop around the world; and the Lockheed Vega piloted
by Amelia Earhart in 1932 in the first solo transatlantic flight
by a woman. Upstairs, the **Albert Einstein Planetarium,**
which charges a small fee, projects images of celestial bod-
ies on a domed ceiling. ⊠ *Jefferson Dr. and 6th St. SW,* ☏
*202/357–2700, TTY 202/357–1729, 202/357–1686 for
movie information.* ☏ *Free.* ☉ *Daily 10–5:30, extended
summer hrs determined annually. Metro: Smithsonian.*

★ ❺ **National Gallery of Art.** The two buildings of the National
Gallery hold one of the world's foremost collections of paintings, sculptures, and graphics. If you want to view the museum's holdings in (more or less) chronological order, it's
best to start your exploration in the **West Building.** Opened
in 1941, the domed West Building was a gift to the nation
from financier Andrew Mellon, who had long collected great
works of art. In 1931, when the Soviet government was short
on cash and selling off many of its art treasures, Mellon
stepped in and bought more than $6 million worth of old
masters, including *The Alba Madonna* by Raphael and
Botticelli's *Adoration of the Magi.* Mellon promised his collection to America in 1936, the year before his death. He
also donated the funds for the construction of the huge
gallery and resisted suggestions it be named after him. The
West Building's **Great Rotunda,** with its 24 marble columns
surrounding a fountain topped with a statue of Mercury,
sets the stage for the masterpieces on display in the more
than 100 separate galleries.

The **East Building** opened in 1978 in response to the changing needs of the National Gallery. The atrium of the East
Building is dominated by Alexander Calder's mobile *Un-
titled.* The galleries here generally display modern art,
though the East Building also serves as a home for major
temporary exhibitions that span years and artistic styles.
Works include Picasso's *The Lovers* and *Family of Saltim-
banques,* four of Matisse's cutouts, Miró's *The Farm,* and
Pollock's *Lavender Mist.* ⊠ *Constitution Ave. between
3rd and 7th Sts. NW,* ☏ *202/737–4215, TTY 202/842–
6176.* ☏ *Free.* ☉ *Mon.–Sat. 10–5, Sun. 11–6. Metro:
Archives/Navy Memorial.*

⓭ **National Museum of African Art.** Founded in 1964 as a private educational institution dedicated to the collection, exhibition, and study of the traditional arts of Africa, this museum now holds more than 7,000 objects representing hundreds of African cultures. On display are masks, carvings, textiles, and jewelry, all made from materials such as wood, fiber, bronze, ivory, and fired clay. One exhibit explores the personal objects—chairs, pipes, cups, snuff containers—that were a part of daily life in 19th- and early 20th-century Africa. ⊠ *950 Independence Ave. SW,* ☎ *202/357–4600, TTY 202/357–4814.* ☎ *Free.* ☉ *Daily 10–5:30. Metro: Smithsonian.*

🖐 ❼ **National Museum of American History.** The incredible diversity of artifacts here helps the Smithsonian live up to its nickname as "the Nation's attic." Visitors can wander for hours on the museum's three floors. The exhibits on the first floor emphasize the history of science and technology. The permanent "Science in American Life" exhibit shows how science has shaped American life through such breakthroughs as the mass production of penicillin, the development of plastics, and the birth of the environmental movement. The second floor is devoted to U.S. social and political history. A permanent exhibit, "First Ladies: Political Role and Public Image," displays the gowns worn by various presidential wives, but it goes beyond fashion to explore the women behind the satin, lace, and brocade. The third floor has installations on ceramics, money, graphic arts, musical instruments, photography, and news reporting. Those who want a more interactive visit should stop at two places: In the **Hands On History Room** visitors can ride a high-wheeler bike, harness a mule, or sort mail as it was done on the railroads in the 1870s. In the **Hands On Science Room** you can perform one of 25 experiments, including testing a water sample and exploring DNA fingerprinting. ⊠ *Constitution Ave. and 14th St. NW,* ☎ *202/357–2700, TTY 202/357–1729.* ☎ *Free.* ☉ *Daily 10–5:30, Hands On History room Tues.–Sun. noon–3, Hands On Science room daily 10–5:30, extended spring and summer hrs determined annually. Metro: Smithsonian.*

★ 🖐 ❻ **National Museum of Natural History.** This is one of the great natural history museums in the world, filled with bones, fossils, stuffed animals, and other natural delights—120 million specimens in all. The first-floor rotunda is dominated by a stuffed, 8-ton, 13-ft African bull elephant, one of the largest ever found. Off to the right is the popular **Dinosaur Hall.** In the west wing are displays of birds, mammals, and sea life. Many of the preserved specimens are from the collection of animals bagged by Teddy Roosevelt on his trips to Africa. If you've always wished you could get your hands on the objects behind the glass, stop by the **Discovery Room,** in the northwest corner of the first floor, where elephant tusks, petrified wood, and other items from the natural world can be handled.

The highlight of the second floor is the **mineral and gem collection.** Objects include the largest sapphire on public display in the country (the Logan Sapphire, 423 carats), the largest uncut diamond (the Oppenheimer Diamond, 253.7 carats), and, of course, the Hope Diamond, a blue gem found in India and reputed to carry a curse (though Smithsonian guides are quick to pooh-pooh this notion). (The Hall of Gems was closed for renovations at press time and was expected to reopen in September 1997.) Also on the second floor is the **O. Orkin Insect Zoo,** where you can view at least 60 species of live insects, from bees to tarantulas. You can even go on hands and knees through a termite mound. ⊠ *Constitution Ave. and 10th St. NW,* ☎ *202/357–2700, TTY 202/357–1729.* ⊑ *Free.* ☉ *Daily 10–5:30; Discovery Room Tues.–Fri. noon–2:30, weekends 10:30–3:30; in spring and summer free passes distributed starting at 11:45 weekdays, 10:15 weekends; extended spring and summer hrs determined annually. Metro: Smithsonian.*

National Sculpture Garden Ice Rink. In winter, you can rent skates at this circular ice-skating rink, which is located across the Mall directly opposite the National Gallery of Art. Ice cream and other refreshments are available at the green building during the summer. ⊠ *7th St. and Constitution Ave. NW,* ☎ *202/371–5340. Metro: Archives/Navy Memorial.*

❶ Smithsonian Institution Building. The first Smithsonian museum constructed, this red sandstone, Norman-style building is better known as the Castle. It was designed by James

Renwick, the architect of St. Patrick's Cathedral in New York City. Although British scientist and founder James Smithson had never visited America, his will stipulated that, should his nephew, Henry James Hungerford, die without an heir, Smithson's entire fortune would go to the United States, "to found at Washington, under the name of the Smithsonian Institution, an establishment for the increase and diffusion of knowledge among men."

Smithson died in 1829, Hungerford in 1835, and in 1838 the United States received $515,169 worth of gold sovereigns. After eight years of congressional debate over the propriety of accepting funds from a private citizen, the Smithsonian Institution was finally established in 1846. The Castle building was completed in 1855 and originally housed all of the Smithsonian's operations, including the science and art collections, research laboratories, and living quarters for the institution's secretary and his family. Smithson's body was brought to America in 1904 and is entombed in a small room to the left of the Castle's Mall entrance.

Today the Castle houses Smithsonian administrative offices and is home to the Woodrow Wilson International School for Scholars. To get your bearings or help in deciding which Mall attractions you want to visit, drop by the **Smithsonian Information Center** in the Castle. A 20-minute video provides an overview of the various Smithsonian museums, and monitors display information on the day's events. Interactive videos provide more detailed information on the museums as well as other attractions in the capital. The Information Center opens at 9 AM, an hour before the other museums open, so you can plan your day on the Mall without wasting valuable sightseeing time. ⊠ *1000 Jefferson Dr. SW,* ☎ *202/357–2700, TTY 202/357–1729.* 🖃 *Free.* ☉ *Daily 9–5:30. Metro: Smithsonian.*

★ ⑧ **United States Holocaust Memorial Museum.** The stories of the 11 million Jews, Gypsies, Jehovah's Witnesses, homosexuals, political prisoners, and others killed by the Nazis between 1933 and 1945 are told here. Striving to give a you-are-there experience, the graphic presentation is as extraordinary as the subject matter: Upon arrival, each visitor is issued an "identity card" containing biographical information on a real person from the Holocaust. As visitors move through the museum, they read sequential updates on their cards. The museum recounts the Holocaust with documentary films, videotaped and audiotaped oral histories, and a collection that includes such items as a German freight car, used to transport Jews from Warsaw to the Treblinka death camp, and the Star of David patches that Jewish prisoners were made to wear. Like the history it covers, the museum can be profoundly disturbing; it is not recommended for visitors under 11. Plan to spend at least four hours here. ⊠ *100 Raoul Wallenberg Pl. SW, enter from Raoul Wallenberg Pl. or 14th St. SW,* ☎ *202/488–0400, 703/218–6500 for Protix.* 🎫 *Free, although same-day timed-entry passes necessary (often not available after 11 AM).* ☉ *Daily 10–5:30. Metro: Smithsonian.*

The Monuments

Washington is a city of monuments. In the middle of traffic circles, on tiny slivers of park, and at street corners and intersections, statues, plaques, and simple blocks of marble honor the generals, politicians, poets, and statesmen who helped shape the nation. The monuments dedicated to the most famous Americans are west of the Mall on ground reclaimed from the marshy flats of the Potomac. This is also the location of Washington's cherry trees, gifts from Japan and focus of a festival each spring.

Numbers in the margin correspond to points of interest on the Monuments map.

Sights to See

❻ Constitution Gardens. Many ideas were proposed to develop a 50-acre site that was once home to "temporary" buildings erected by the Navy before World War I and not removed until after World War II. President Nixon is said to have favored something resembling Copenhagen's Tivoli Gardens. The final design was a little plainer, with paths winding through groves of trees and, on the lake, a tiny island paying tribute to the signers of the Declaration of Independence, their signatures carved into a low stone wall. ⊠ *Constitution Ave. between 17th and 23rd Sts. NW. Metro: Foggy Bottom.*

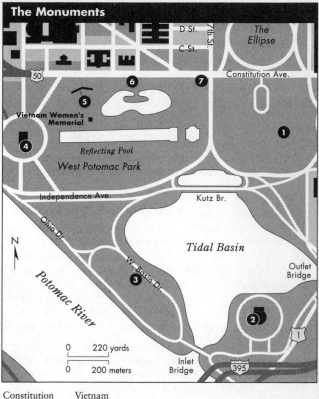

The Monuments

Constitution Gardens, **6**

Franklin Delano Roosevelt Memorial, **3**

Jefferson Memorial, **2**

Lincoln Memorial, **4**

Lockkeeper's House, **7**

Vietnam Veterans Memorial, **5**

Washington Monument, **1**

❸ **Franklin Delano Roosevelt Memorial.** This is the District's newest monument, unveiled in May 1997. The controversial 7.5-acre memorial to the 32nd president features waterfalls and reflection pools, four outdoor gallery rooms—each symbolizing one of his four terms as president—and 10 bronze sculptures. The granite passageways that connect the galleries are engraved with some of Roosevelt's most famous quotes, including "The only thing we have to fear is fear itself." ✉ *West side of Tidal Basin,* ☎ *202/619–7222.* 🎫 *Free.* ☉ *24 hrs.; staffed daily 8 AM–midnight.*

❷ **Jefferson Memorial.** Congress decided that Jefferson deserved a monument positioned as prominently as those in honor of Washington and Lincoln, and this spot directly south of the White House seemed ideal. Jefferson had always admired the Pantheon in Rome—the rotundas he designed for the University of Virginia and his own Monticello were inspired by its dome—so architect John Russell Pope drew from the same source when he designed this memorial. Dedicated in 1943, it houses a statue of Jefferson, and its walls are lined with inscriptions based on his writings. One of the best views of the White House can be seen from the memorial's top steps. ✉ *Tidal Basin, south bank,* ☎ *202/426–6821.* 🎫 *Free.* ☉ *Daily 8 AM–midnight. Metro: Smithsonian.*

★ ❹ **Lincoln Memorial.** This white Colorado-marble memorial was designed by Henry Bacon and completed in 1922. The 36 Doric columns represent the 36 states in the Union at the time of Lincoln's death; the names of the states appear on the frieze above the columns. Above the frieze are the names of the 48 states in the Union when the memorial was dedicated. (Alaska and Hawaii are noted by an inscription on the terrace leading up to the memorial.) Daniel Chester French's somber statue of the seated president, in the center of the memorial, gazes out over the Reflecting Pool. Though the 19-ft-high sculpture looks as if it were cut from one huge block of stone, it actually comprises 28 interlocking pieces of Georgia marble. Inscribed on the south wall is the Gettysburg Address, and on the north wall is Lincoln's second inaugural address. Above each inscription is a mural painted by Jules Guerine. The memorial served as a fitting backdrop for Martin Luther King's "I have a dream" speech in 1963.

Many visitors look only at the front and inside of the Lincoln Memorial, but there is much more to explore. On the lower level to the left is a display that chronicles the memorial's construction. There is also a set of windows that look onto the huge structure's foundation. Although visiting the area around the Lincoln Memorial during the day allows you to take in an impressive view of the Mall to the east, the best time to see the memorial itself is at night. Spotlights illuminate the outside while inside, light and shadows play across Lincoln's gentle face. ⊠ *West end of Mall,* ☎ *202/426–6895.* 🖼 *Free.* ☾ *24 hrs; staffed daily 8 AM– midnight. Metro: Foggy Bottom.*

❼ Lockkeeper's House. The stone Lockkeeper's House is the only remaining monument to Washington's unsuccessful experiment with a canal. L'Enfant's design called for a canal to be dug from the Tiber—a branch of the Potomac that extended from where the Lincoln Memorial is now—across the city to the Capitol and then south to the Anacostia River. The City Canal became more nuisance than convenience, and by the Civil War it was a foul-smelling cesspool that often overran its banks. The stone building at this corner was the home of the canal's lockkeeper until the 1870s, when the waterway was covered over with B Street, which was renamed Constitution Avenue in 1932. ⊠ *Constitution Ave. and 17th St. Metro: Federal Triangle, 5 blocks east on 12th St.*

�!️ Tidal Basin. This placid pond was part of the Potomac until 1882, when portions of the river were filled in to improve navigation and create additional parkland, including that upon which the Jefferson Memorial was later built. Paddleboats have been a fixture on the Tidal Basin for years. You can rent one at the boathouse on the east side of the basin, southwest of the Bureau of Engraving. Look for the bronze sculptures, two human-headed fish that spout water, under Inlet Bridge, on the south side of the basin. They were designed in honor of the chief of the park, Jack Fish.

Once you cross the Inlet Bridge, you have a choice: You can walk to the left, along the Potomac, or continue along the Tidal Basin to the right. The latter route is somewhat more scenic, especially when the cherry trees are in bloom. The first batch of these trees arrived from Japan in 1909. The trees were infected with insects and fungus, however, and the Department of Agriculture ordered them destroyed. A diplomatic crisis was averted when the United States politely asked the Japanese for another batch, and in 1912 Mrs. William Howard Taft planted the first tree. The second was planted by the wife of the Japanese ambassador. The trees are now the centerpiece of Washington's Cherry Blossom Festival held each spring; they're usually in bloom for about 10–12 days at the beginning of April. ⊠ *Boathouse: Northeast bank of Tidal Basin,* ☎ *202/479–2426.* 💵 *Paddleboat rental $7 per hr, $1.75 each additional 15 mins.* ☉ *Mid-Mar.–Oct., daily 10–6 (until 5 in Mar. and Apr.), weather permitting. Metro: Smithsonian.*

⑤ **Vietnam Veterans Memorial.** Renowned for its power to evoke deep and poignant reflection, the Vietnam Veterans Memorial was conceived by Jan Scruggs, a former infantry corporal who had served in Vietnam. The stark design by Maya Ying Lin, a 21-year-old Yale architecture student, was selected in a 1981 competition. The names of more than 58,000 Americans are etched on the face of the memorial in the order of their deaths. Directories at the entrance and exit to the wall list the names in alphabetical order. For help in finding a specific name, ask a ranger at the blue-and-white hut near the entrance. Thousands of offerings are left at the wall each year: letters, flowers, medals, uniforms, snapshots. The National Park Service collects these and stores them in a warehouse in Lanham, Maryland, where they are fast becoming another memorial. Tents are often set up near the wall by veterans groups; some provide information on soldiers who remain missing in action, and others are on call to help fellow vets deal with the sometimes overwhelming emotions that grip them when visiting the wall for the first time. ⊠ *Constitution Gardens, 23rd St. and Constitution Ave. NW,* ☎ *202/634–1568.* 💵 *Free.* ☉ *24 hrs; staffed daily 8 AM–midnight. Metro: Foggy Bottom.*

Vietnam Women's Memorial. After years of debate, the Vietnam Women's Memorial, honoring the women who served in that conflict, was finally dedicated on Veterans Day 1993. It is a stirring sculpture group consisting of two uniformed women caring for a wounded male soldier while a third woman kneels nearby. ⊠ *Constitution Gardens, southeast of Vietnam Veterans Memorial. Metro: Foggy Bottom.*

○ **❶ Washington Monument.** Congress first authorized a monument to General Washington in 1783. In his 1791 plan for
the city, Pierre L'Enfant selected a site (the point where a line
drawn west from the Capitol crossed one drawn south from
the White House), but it wasn't until 1833, after years of quib-
bling in Congress, that a private National Monument Society was formed to select a designer and to search for funds.
Robert Mills's winning design called for a 600-ft-tall decorated obelisk rising from a circular colonnaded building.
The building at the base was to be an American pantheon,
adorned with statues of national heroes and a massive statue
of Washington riding in a chariot pulled by snorting horses.

Because of the marshy conditions of L'Enfant's original site,
the position of the monument was shifted to firmer ground
100 yards southeast. (If you walk a few steps north of the
monument you can see the stone marker that denotes L'Enfant's original axis.) The cornerstone was laid in 1848 with
the same Masonic trowel Washington himself had used to
lay the Capitol's cornerstone 55 years earlier. The Monument Society continued to raise funds after construction was
begun, soliciting subscriptions of one dollar from citizens
across America. It also urged states, organizations, and
foreign governments to contribute memorial stones for the
construction. Problems arose in 1854, when members of
the anti-Papist "Know Nothing" party stole a block donated
by Pope Pius IX, smashed it, and dumped its shards into
the Potomac. This action, a lack of funds, and the onset of
the Civil War kept the monument at a fraction of its final
height, open at the top, and vulnerable to the rain. A clearly
visible ring about a third of the way up the obelisk testi-
fies to this unfortunate stage of the monument's history.

In 1876 Congress finally appropriated $200,000 to finish
the monument, and the Army Corps of Engineers took
over construction—work was finally completed in December 1884. The Washington Monument is the world's
tallest masonry structure. The view from the top takes in
most of the District and parts of Maryland and Virginia.
To avoid the formerly long lines of people waiting for the
minute-long elevator ride up the monument's shaft, the Park
Service now uses a free timed-ticket system. A limited number of tickets are available at the kiosk on 15th Street daily

beginning at 7:30 AM April–Labor Day and 8:30 AM September–March, with a limit of six tickets per person. Tickets are good during a specified half-hour period. No tickets are required after 8 PM (3 PM in the off-season). Advance tickets are available from Ticketmaster (☎ 202/432–7328). There is a $1.50 per ticket service charge when using Ticketmaster. ⊠ *Constitution Ave. and 15th St. NW,* ☎ *202/426–6840.* ☒ *Free.* ☉ *Apr.–Labor Day, daily 8 AM–midnight; Sept.–Mar., daily 9–5. Metro: Smithsonian.*

The White House Area

In a world full of immediately recognizable images, few are better known—not just in the U.S. but from Chile to China—than the whitewashed, 32-room, Irish country house-like mansion at 1600 Pennsylvania Avenue, the country's most famous address, known as the White House. The residence of arguably the single most powerful person on the planet, it has an awesome majesty, having been the home of every U.S. president but, ironically, the father of our country, George Washington. After joining the more than 1.5 million people who visit the White House each year, strike out into the surrounding streets to explore the president's neighborhood, which includes some of the oldest houses in the city.

Numbers in the margin correspond to points of interest on the White House Area map.

Sights to See

American Red Cross. Though it hosts occasional art exhibits, the American Red Cross national headquarters is mainly of passing interest. It's composed of three buildings. The primary building, a neoclassic structure of blinding white marble built in 1917, commemorates the service and devotion of the women who cared for the wounded on both sides during the Civil War. The building's Georgian-style board of governors hall has three stained-glass windows designed by Louis Tiffany. ⊠ *430 17th St. NW,* ☎ *202/737–8300.* ☒ *Free.* ☉ *Weekdays 9–4. Metro: Farragut West.*

⓭ **Art Museum of the Americas.** This small gallery has changing exhibits highlighting 20th-century Latin American artists. ⊠ *201 18th St. NW,* ☎ *202/458–6016.* ☒ *Free.* ☉ *Tues.–Sat. 10–5. Metro: Farragut West.*

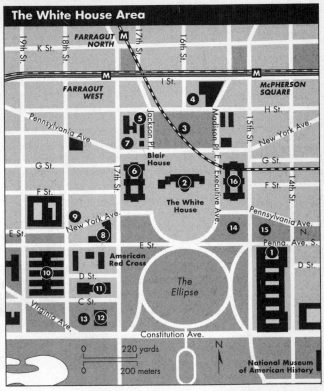

The White House Area

FARRAGUT NORTH

K St.

19th St. · 18th St. · 17th St. · 16th St.

FARRAGUT WEST

McPHERSON SQUARE

I St.

Pennsylvania Ave.

Jackson Pl.

Madison Pl.

H St.

New York Ave.

15th St.

④

③

⑤

⑦

G St.

Blair House

G St.

F St.

⑥

②

14th St.

⑯

F St.

17th St.

The White House

Executive Ave.

⑨

New York Ave.

Pennsylvania Ave.

E St.

⑧

⑭

⑮

N.

E St.

Penna. Ave. S.

American Red Cross

①

D St.

⑩

D St.

The Ellipse

⑪

C St.

Virginia Ave.

⑬ ⑫

Constitution Ave.

N

0   220 yards
0   200 meters

National Museum of American History

Art Museum of the Americas, **13**

Corcoran Gallery of Art, **8**

DAR Museum, **11**

Decatur House, **5**

Department of the Interior, **10**

Lafayette Square, **3**

Octagon, **9**

Old Executive Office Building, **6**

Organization of American States, **12**

Pershing Park, **15**

Renwick Gallery, **7**

St. John's Episcopal Church, **4**

Treasury Building, **16**

White House, **2**

White House Visitor Center, **1**

William Tecumseh Sherman Monument, **14**

Blair House. A green canopy marks the entrance to Blair House, the residence used by heads of state visiting Washington. Harry S. Truman lived here from 1948 to 1952 while the White House was undergoing its much-needed renovation. A plaque on the fence honors White House policeman Leslie Coffelt, who died in 1950 when Puerto Rican separatists attempted to assassinate President Truman at this site. ✉ *1651 Pennsylvania Ave. Metro: McPherson Square.*

❽ Corcoran Gallery of Art. The Corcoran is one of the few large museums in Washington outside the Smithsonian family. The beaux arts–style building, its copper roof green with age, was designed by Ernest Flagg and completed in 1897. The gallery's permanent collection numbers more than 11,000 works, including paintings by the first great American portraitists John Copley, Gilbert Stuart, and Rembrandt Peale. The Hudson River School is represented by such works as *Mount Corcoran* by Albert Bierstadt and Frederic Church's *Niagara.* There are also portraits by John Singer Sargent, Thomas Eakins, and Mary Cassatt. European art is seen in the Walker Collection (late-19th- and early 20th-century paintings, including works by Courbet, Monet, Pissarro, and Renoir) and the Clark Collection (Dutch, Flemish, and French Romantic paintings, and the restored entire 18th-century Salon Doré of the Hotel d'Orsay in Paris). Be sure to see Samuel Morse's *Old House of Representatives* and Hiram Powers's *Greek Slave,* which scandalized Victorian society. Photography and works by contemporary American artists are also among the Corcoran's strengths. ✉ *500 17th St. NW,* ☎ *202/639–1700.* 🎟 *Suggested donation: $3.* ☉ *Mon., Wed., and Fri.–Sun. 10–5; Thurs. 10–9; tours of permanent collection Mon.–Wed. and Fri. at noon, Sat.–Sun. at 10:30 AM, noon, and 2:30 PM, Thurs. at 7:30 PM. Metro: Farragut West.*

☞ ⓫ DAR Museum. A beaux arts building serving as headquarters of the Daughters of the American Revolution, Memorial Continental Hall was the site each year of the DAR's congress until the larger Constitution Hall was built around the corner. An entrance on D Street leads to the DAR Museum. Its 50,000-item collection includes fine examples of Colonial and Federal silver, china, porcelain, stoneware, earthenware, and glass. Thirty-three period rooms are decorated in styles representative of various U.S. states, ranging from an 1850 California adobe parlor to a New Hampshire attic filled with toys from the 18th and 19th centuries. Docents are available for tours weekdays 10–2:30 and Sunday 1–5. Kids will especially love the "Colonial Adventure" tours that are usually held the first and third Sundays of the month. Make reservations at least 10 days in advance by calling 202/879–3241. ⊠ *1776 D St. NW,* ☎ *202/879–3240.* ☎ *Free.* ☉ *Weekdays 8:30–4, Sun. 1–5. Metro: Farragut West.*

❺ Decatur House. Designed by Benjamin Latrobe, Decatur House was built for naval hero Stephen Decatur and his wife Susan in 1819. A redbrick, Federal-style building on the corner of H Street and Jackson Place, it was the first private residence on President's Park (the White House doesn't really count as *private*). Decatur had earned the affection of the nation in battles against the British and the Barbary pirates. He used the prize money Congress awarded him for his exploits to build this home near the White House. Tragically, only 14 months after he moved in, Decatur was killed in a duel with James Barron, a disgruntled former Navy officer who held Decatur responsible for his court-martial. Later occupants of the house included Henry Clay, Martin Van Buren, and the Beales, a prominent family from the West whose modifications of the building include a parquet floor showing the state seal of California. The house is now operated by the National Trust. The first floor is furnished as it was in Decatur's time. The second floor is furnished in the Victorian style favored by the Beale family, who owned it until 1956 (thus making Decatur House both the first and *last* private residence on Lafayette Square). ⊠ *748 Jackson Pl. NW,* ☎ *202/842–0920.* ☎ *$4.* ☉ *Tues.–Fri. 10–3, weekends noon–4; tours on the hr and ½ hr. Metro: Farragut West.*

❿ Department of the Interior. Designed by Waddy B. Wood, the Department of the Interior building was the most modern government building in the city and the first with escalators and central air-conditioning at the time of its construction in 1937. The outside of the building is somewhat plain, but much of the interior is decorated with paintings that reflect the Interior Department's work. Hallways feature heroic oil paintings of dam construction, panning for gold, and cattle drives. You'll pass several of these if you visit the **Department of the Interior Museum** on the first floor. (You can enter the building at its E Street or C Street doors; adults must show photo ID.) The small museum tells the story of the Department of the Interior, a huge agency dubbed the "Mother of Departments" because from it grew the Departments of Agriculture, Labor, Education, and Energy. Today Interior oversees most of the country's federally owned land and natural resources, and exhibits in the museum outline the work done by the Bureau of Land Management, the U.S. Geological Survey, the Bureau of Indian Affairs, the National Park Service, and other Interior branches. Call at least two weeks ahead to schedule a tour of the building's architecture and murals. ⊠ *C and E Sts. between 18th and 19th Sts. NW,* ☎ *202/208–4743.* ▱ *Free.* ☉ *Weekdays 8–5. Metro: Farragut West.*

❸ **Lafayette Square.** L'Enfant's original plan for the city designated this area as part of "President's Park"; in essence it was the president's front yard. The egalitarian Thomas Jefferson, concerned that large, landscaped White House grounds would give the wrong impression in a democratic country, ordered that the area be turned into a public park. Soldiers camped in the square during the War of 1812 and the Civil War, turning it at both times into a muddy pit. Today, protesters set their placards up in Lafayette Square, jockeying for positions that face the White House.

In the center of the park is a large **statue of Andrew Jackson.** Erected in 1853 and cast from bronze cannon that Jackson had captured during the War of 1812, this was the first equestrian statue made in America. Jackson's is the only statue of an American in the park. The other statues represent foreign-born soldiers who helped in America's fight for independence. In the southeast corner is the park's namesake, the **Marquis de Lafayette,** the young French nobleman who came to America to fight in the Revolution. The colonnaded building across Madison Place at the corner of Pennsylvania Avenue is an annex to the Treasury Department. The modern redbrick building farther on, at 717 Madison Place, houses a variety of judicial offices. Its design—with the squared-off bay windows—is echoed in the taller building that rises behind it and is mirrored in the **New Executive Office Building** on the other side of Lafayette Square. The next house down, yellow with a second-story ironwork balcony, was built in 1828 by Benjamin Ogle Tayloe. During the McKinley administration, Ohio Senator Marcus Hanna lived here, and the president's frequent visits earned it the nickname the "Little White House." ⊠ *Bounded by Pennsylvania Ave., Madison Pl., H St., and Jackson Pl. Metro: McPherson Square.*

⑨ Octagon. This octagon actually has six, rather than eight, sides. Designed by William Thornton (the Capitol's architect), it was built for John Tayloe III, a wealthy Virginia plantation owner and was completed in 1801. After the White House was burned in 1814 the Tayloes invited James and Dolley Madison to stay in the Octagon. It was in a second-floor study that the Treaty of Ghent, ending the War of 1812, was signed. By the late 1800s the building was used as a rooming house. In this century the house served as the headquarters of the American Institute of Architects before the construction of AIA's rather unexceptional building behind it. It is now the **museum of the American Architectural Foundation.** The galleries inside host changing exhibits on architecture, city planning, and Washington history and design. ⊠ *1799 New York Ave. NW,* ☎ *202/638–3105, TTY 202/638–1538.* ▣ *$3.* ☉ *Tues.—Sun. 10–4. Metro: Farragut West.*

⑥ Old Executive Office Building. Once one of the most detested buildings in the city, the Old Executive Office Building is now one of the most beloved. It was built between 1871 and 1888 and originally housed the War, Navy, and State departments. Its architect, Alfred B. Mullett, patterned it after the Louvre, but detractors quickly criticized the busy French Empire design—with its mansard roof, tall chimneys, and 900 freestanding columns—as an inappropriate counterpoint to the Greek Revival Treasury Building that sits on the other side of the White House. Numerous plans to alter the facade foundered due to lack of money. The granite edifice may look like a wedding cake, but its high ceilings and spacious offices make it popular with occupants, who include members of the executive branch. Dan Quayle had his office in here; Albert Gore Jr. is a little closer to the

action, in the West Wing of the White House, just down
the hall from the president. The Old Executive Office Building has played host to numerous historic events. It was here
that Secretary of State Cordell Hull met with Japanese
diplomats after the bombing of Pearl Harbor, and it was
here that Oliver North and Fawn Hall shredded Iran-
Contra documents. ⊠ *Across Pennsylvania Ave. west of
White House. Metro: Farragut West.*

⑫ **Organization of American States.** The headquarters of the
Organization of American States contains a cool patio
adorned with a pre-Columbian–style fountain and lush tropical plants. This tiny rain forest is a good place to rest
when Washington's summer heat is at its most oppressive.
The upstairs Hall of Flags and Heroes contains, as the
name implies, busts of generals and statesmen from the various OAS member countries as well as each country's flag.
⊠ *17th St. and Constitution Ave. NW,* ☎ *202/458–3000.*
▣ *Free.* ☉ *Weekdays 9–5:30. Metro: Farragut West.*

⑮ **Pershing Park.** A quiet sunken garden honors General
"Blackjack" Pershing, famed for his failed attempt to cap-
ture the Mexican revolutionary Pancho Villa in 1916-1917
and then for commanding the American expeditionary
force in World War I, among other military exploits. En-
gravings on the stone walls recount pivotal campaigns
from that war. Ice-skaters glide on the square pool in the
winter. ⊠ *15th St. and Pennsylvania Ave. Metro: McPherson Square.*

➐ **Renwick Gallery.** The French Second Empire–style building was designed by Smithsonian Castle architect James Renwick in 1859 to house the art collection of Washington
merchant and banker William Wilson Corcoran. Corcoran
was a Southern sympathizer who spent the duration of the
Civil War in Europe. While he was away his unfinished building was pressed into service by the government as a quar-
termaster general's post. In 1874 the Corcoran, as it was
then called, opened as the first private art museum in the
city. Corcoran's collection quickly outgrew the building and
in 1897 it was moved to a new gallery a few blocks south
on 17th Street (☞ Corcoran Gallery of Art, *above*). After
a stint as the U.S. Court of Claims, the building was restored,
renamed after its architect, and opened in 1972 as the

Smithsonian's museum of American decorative arts—today it's at the forefront of the crafts movement. Not everything in the museum is Shaker furniture and enamel jewelry, though. The second-floor Grand Salon is still furnished in the opulent Victorian style Corcoran favored when his collection adorned its walls. ⊠ *Pennsylvania Ave. and 17th St. NW, ☎ 202/357–2700, TTY 202/357–1729. ☞ Free. ☉ Daily 10–5:30. Metro: McPherson Square.*

❹ **St. John's Episcopal Church.** The golden-domed, so-called "Church of the Presidents" sits directly across Lafayette Park from the White House. Every president since Madison has visited the church, and many worshiped here on a regular basis. Built in 1816, the church was the second building on the square. Benjamin Latrobe, who worked on both the Capitol and the White House, designed it in the form of a Greek cross, with a flat dome and a lantern cupola. The church has been altered somewhat since then; later additions include the Doric portico and the cupola tower. Not far from the center of the church is pew 54, where visiting presidents are seated. The kneelers of many of the pews are embroidered with the presidential seal and the names of several chief executives. ⊠ *16th and H Sts. NW, ☎ 202/347–8766. ☞ Free. ☉ Mon.–Sat. 9–3, tours after 11 AM Sun. service the first Sun. of each month and by appointment. Metro: McPherson Square.*

⑯ **Treasury Building.** Construction of the Treasury Building started in 1836 and, after several additions, was finally completed in 1869. Robert Mills, the architect responsible for the Washington Monument and the Patent Office (now the National Museum of American Art), designed the grand colonnade that stretches down 15th Street. The southern facade of the Treasury Building has a **statue of Alexander Hamilton,** the department's first secretary. Guided 90-minute tours are given every Saturday, except holiday weekends, at 10, 10:20, 10:40, and 11, and take visitors past the Andrew Johnson suite, used by Johnson as the executive office while Mrs. Lincoln moved out of the White House; the two-story marble Cash Room; and a 19th-century burglarproof vault lining that saw duty when the Treasury stored currency. Register at least one week ahead for the tour; visitors must provide name, date of birth, and

Social Security number and must show a photo ID at the
start of the tour. ✉ *15th St. and Pennsylvania Ave. NW,*
☎ *202/622–0896, TTY 202/622–0692.* ✍ *Free. Metro:
McPherson Square.*

★ ☝ ❷ **White House.** Pierre L'Enfant called it the President's House;
it was known formally as the Executive Mansion; and in
1902 Congress officially proclaimed it the White House,
though, contrary to popular belief, it had been given that
nickname even before its white sandstone exterior was
painted to cover the fire damage it suffered during the War
of 1812. Irishman James Hoban's plan, based on the Georgian design of Leinster Hall in Dublin and of other Irish
country houses, was selected in a contest, in 1792. The building wasn't ready for its first occupant, John Adams, the second U.S. president, until 1800, and so, in a colossal irony,
George Washington, who seems to have slept everyplace
else, never slept here. Completed in 1829, it has undergone
many structural changes since then: Thomas Jefferson,
who had entered his own design in the contest under an
assumed name, added terraces to the east and west wings.
Andrew Jackson installed running water. James Garfield put
in the first elevator. Between 1948 and 1952, Harry Truman had the entire structure gutted and restored, adding
a second-story porch to the south portico. George Bush installed a horseshoe pit. Most recently, Bill Clinton had a
customized jogging track put in.

Tuesday through Saturday mornings (except holidays),
from 10 AM to noon, selected public rooms on the ground
floor and first floor of the White House are open to visitors. There are two ways to visit the White House. The most
popular (and easiest) way is to pick up timed tickets from
the White House Visitor Center. Plan on being there 5–10
minutes before your tour is scheduled to begin. The other
option is to write to your representative or senator's office
8–10 weeks in advance of your trip to request special VIP
passes for tours between 8 and 10 AM, but these tickets are
extremely limited. On selected weekends in April and October, the White House is open for garden tours. In December
it's decorated for the holidays.

You'll enter the White House through the East Wing lobby
on the ground floor, past the Jacqueline Kennedy Rose

Garden. Your first stop is the large white-and-gold **East Room,** the site of presidential news conferences. In 1814 Dolley Madison saved the room's full-length portrait of George Washington from torch-carrying British soldiers by cutting it from its frame, rolling it up, and spiriting it out of the White House. (No fool she, Dolley also rescued her own portrait.) A later occupant, Teddy Roosevelt, allowed his children to ride their pet pony in the East Room.

The Federal-style **Green Room,** named for the moss-green watered silk that covers its walls, is used for informal receptions and "photo opportunities" with foreign heads of state. The president and his guests are often shown on TV sitting in front of the Green Room's English Empire mantel, engaging in what are invariably described as "frank and cordial" discussions.

The elliptical **Blue Room,** the most formal space in the White House, is furnished with a gilded Empire-style settee and chairs ordered by James Monroe. (Monroe asked for plain wooden chairs, but the furniture manufacturer thought such unadorned furnishings too simple for the White House.) Another well-known elliptical room, the president's **Oval Office,** is in the semidetached West Wing of the White House, along with other executive offices. The **Red Room** is decorated as an American Empire–style parlor of the early 19th century, with furniture by the New York cabinetmaker Charles-Honoré Lannuier. The **State Dining Room,** second in size only to the East Room, can seat 140 guests. The room is dominated by G. P. A. Healy's portrait of Abraham Lincoln, painted after the president's death. The stone mantel is inscribed with a quotation from one of John Adams's letters: "I pray heaven to bestow the best of blessings on this house and all that shall hereafter inhabit it. May none but honest and wise men ever rule under this roof." In Teddy Roosevelt's day a stuffed moose head hung over the mantel. ✉ *1600 Pennsylvania Ave. NW,* ☎ *202/ 456–7041 or 202/619–7222.* 🎟 *Free.* ☉ *Tues.–Sat. 10– noon. Metro: Federal Triangle.*

❶ White House Visitor Center. If you're visiting the White House, you'll need to stop by the visitor center for free tickets. Tickets are dispensed on a first-come, first-served basis. (They are often gone by 9 AM.) Your ticket will show the starting point and approximate time of your tour. Also at the center are exhibits pertaining to the White House's construction, its decor, and the families who have lived there. Photographs, artifacts, and videos relate the house's history to those who don't have the opportunity to tour the building personally. ✉ *Official address: 1450 Pennsylvania Avenue NW; entrance: Commerce Department's Baldrige Hall, E St. between 14th and 15th Sts.,* ☎ *202/208–1631.* 🎫 *Free.* ☉ *Daily 7:30–4. Metro: Federal Triangle.*

⑭ **William Tecumseh Sherman Monument.** Sherman, whose Atlanta Campaign in 1864 cut a bloody swath of destruction through the Confederacy, was said to be the greatest Civil War general, as the sheer size of this massive monument, set in a small park, would seem to attest. ✉ *Bounded by E and 15th Sts., East Executive Ave., and Alexander Hamilton Pl. Metro: Federal Triangle.*

Capitol Hill

The people who live and work on "the Hill" do so in the shadow of the edifice that lends the neighborhood its name: the gleaming white Capitol building. More than just the center of government, the Hill includes charming residential blocks lined with Victorian row houses and a fine assortment of restaurants, bars, and shops. Capitol Hill's boundaries are disputed: It's bordered to the west, north, and south by the Capitol, Union Station, and I Street, respectively. Some argue that Capitol Hill extends east to the Anacostia River, others that it ends at 11th Street near Lincoln Park. The neighborhood does in fact seem to grow as members of Capitol Hill's active historic-preservation movement restore more and more 19th-century houses.

Numbers in the margin correspond to points of interest on the Capitol Hill map.

Sights to See

⑨ **Bartholdi Fountain.** Frédéric-Auguste Bartholdi, sculptor of the more famous—and much larger—Statue of Liberty, created this delightful fountain, some 25 ft tall, for the Philadelphia Centennial Exhibition of 1876. With its aquatic monsters, sea nymphs, tritons, and lighted globes (once gas, now electric), the fountain represents the elements of water and light. The U.S. Government purchased the fountain after the exhibition and placed it on the grounds of the old Botanic Garden on the Mall. It was moved to its present location in 1932. ⊠ *1st St. and Independence Ave. SW. Metro: Federal Center.*

★ ⟲ ❹ **Capitol.** As beautiful as the building itself are the Capitol grounds, landscaped in the late-19th century by Frederick Law Olmsted, who, along with Calvert Vaux, created New York City's Central Park. On these 68 acres you will find both the tamest squirrels in the city and the highest concentration of television news correspondents, jockeying for a good position in front of the Capitol for their "stand-ups."

The design of this monument was the result of a competition held in 1792; the winner was William Thornton, a physician and amateur architect from the West Indies. The cornerstone was laid by George Washington in a Masonic ceremony on September 18, 1793, and in November 1800, both the Senate and the House of Representatives moved down from Philadelphia to occupy the first completed section of the Capitol: the boxlike portion between the central rotunda and today's north wing. By 1806 the House wing had been completed, just to the south of what is now the domed center, and a covered wooden walkway joined the two wings.

The Congress House grew slowly and suffered a grave setback on August 24, 1814, when British troops led by Sir George Cockburn marched on Washington and set fire to the Capitol, the White House, and numerous other government buildings. The wooden walkway was destroyed and the two wings gutted, but the walls were left standing after a violent rainstorm doused the flames. Architect Benjamin Henry Latrobe supervised the rebuilding of the Capitol, adding such American touches as the corn-cob-and-tobacco-leaf capitals to columns in the east entrance to the Senate wing. He was followed by Boston-born Charles Bulfinch, and in 1826 the Capitol, its low wooden dome sheathed in copper, was finally finished.

North and south wings were added in the 1850s and '60s to accommodate a growing government trying to keep

Capitol Hill

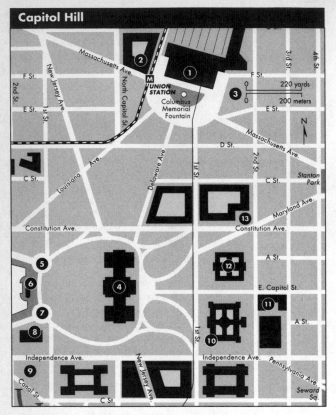

Bartholdi Fountain, **9**

Capitol, **4**

Folger Shakespeare Library, **11**

Grant Memorial, **6**

James Garfield Memorial, **7**

Library of Congress, **10**

National Postal Museum, **2**

Peace Monument, **5**

Sewall-Belmont House, **13**

Supreme Court Building, **12**

Thurgood Marshall Federal Judiciary Building, **3**

Union Station, **1**

United States Botanic Garden, **8**

pace with a growing country. The elongated edifice extended
farther north and south than Thornton had planned, and
in 1855, to keep the scale correct, work began on a tall cast-
iron dome. President Lincoln was criticized for continuing
this expensive project while the country was in the throes
of the Civil War, but he called the construction "a sign we
intend the Union shall go on." The figure on top of the dome,
often mistaken for Pocahontas, is called *Freedom*.

Guided tours of the Capitol usually start beneath the dome
in the Rotunda, but if there's a crowd you may have to wait
in a line that forms at the top of the center steps on the east
side. If you want to forgo the tour, which is brief but in-
formative, you may look around on your own. Enter
through one of the lower doors to the right or left of the
main steps. Start your exploration under Constantino Brumidi's *Apotheosis of Washington,* the fresco in the center
of the dome, completed in 1865. The flat, sculpture-style
frieze around the rim of the Rotunda depicting 400 years
of American history was started by Brumidi. While painting Penn's treaty with the Indians, the 74-year-old artist
slipped on the 58-ft-high scaffold and almost fell off. Brumidi managed to hang on until help arrived, but he died a
few months later from shock brought on by the incident.
The work was continued by another Italian, Filippo Costag-
gini, but the frieze wasn't finished until American Allyn Cox
added the final touches in 1953.

Notice the Rotunda's eight immense oil paintings of scenes
from American history. The four scenes from the Revolutionary War are by John Trumbull, who served alongside
George Washington and painted the first president from life.
Twenty-six people have lain in state in the Rotunda, including
nine presidents, from Abraham Lincoln to Lyndon Baines
Johnson. Underneath the Rotunda, above an empty crypt
that was designed to hold the remains of George and
Martha Washington, is an exhibit chronicling the construction of the Capitol.

South of the Rotunda is Statuary Hall, once the legislative
chamber of the House of Representatives. When the House
moved out, Congress invited each state to send statues of
two great deceased citizens for placement in the former cham-

ber. Because the weight of the accumulated statues threatened to cave the floor in, some of the sculptures were dispersed to various other spots throughout the Capitol. To the north, on the Senate side, you can look into the chamber once used by the Supreme Court and into the splendid Old Senate Chamber above it, both of which have been restored. Also be sure to see the Brumidi Corridor on the ground floor of the Senate wing. The Italian artist also memorialized several American heroes, painting them inside trompe l'oeil frames. Trusting that America would continue to produce heroes long after he was gone, Brumidi left some frames empty. The most recent one to be filled, in 1987, honors the crew of the space shuttle *Challenger*.

If you want to watch some of the legislative action in the **House or Senate chambers** while you're on the Hill you'll have to get a gallery pass from the office of your representative or senator. (To find out where those offices are, ask any Capitol police officer, or call 202/224–3121.) In the chambers you'll notice that Democrats sit to the right of the presiding officer, Republicans to the left—the opposite, it's often noted, of their political leanings. The *Washington Post*'s daily "Today in Congress" lists when and where the committees are meeting. To get to a House or Senate office building, go to the Capitol's basement and ride the miniature subway used by legislators.

When you're finished exploring the inside of the Capitol, make your way to the **west side.** In 1981 Ronald Reagan broke with tradition and moved the presidential swearing-in ceremony to this side of the Capitol, which offers a dramatic view of the Mall and monuments below and can accommodate more guests than the east side, where all previous presidents took the oath of office. ⊠ *East end of Mall,* ☎ *202/224– 3121 or 202/225–6827 (guide service).* ☒ *Free.* ☉ *Daily 9– 4:30; summer hrs determined annually, but Rotunda and Statuary Hall usually open daily 9:30–8. Metro: Capitol South or Union Station.*

⓫ **Folger Shakespeare Library.** The Folger Library's collection of works by and about Shakespeare and his times is second to none. The white-marble Art Deco building, designed by architect Paul Philippe Cret, is decorated with scenes from the Bard's plays. Inside is a reproduction of an inn-yard theater, which is the setting for performances of chamber music, baroque opera, and other events appropriate to the surroundings, and a gallery, designed in the manner of an Elizabethan Great Hall, which hosts rotating exhibits from the library's collection. ⊠ *201 E. Capitol St. SE,* ☎ *202/544–4600.* ⊠ *Free.* ☉ *Mon.–Sat. 10–4. Metro: Capitol South.*

⑥ Grant Memorial. The 252-ft-long memorial to the 16th American president and commander in chief of the Union forces during the Civil War is the largest sculpture group in the city. The statue of Ulysses S. Grant on horseback is flanked by Union artillery and cavalry. ⊠ *Near 1st St. and Maryland Ave. SW. Metro: Federal Center.*

⑦ James Garfield Memorial. Near the Grant Memorial and the United States Botanic Gardens is a memorial to the 20th president of the United States. James Garfield was assassinated in 1881 after only a few months in office. His bronze statue stands on a pedestal with three other bronze figures seated around it; one bears a tablet inscribed with the words "Law," "Justice," and "Prosperity," which the figures presumably represent. ⊠ *1st St. and Maryland Ave. SW. Metro: Federal Center.*

⑩ Library of Congress. Provisions for a library to serve members of Congress were originally made in 1800, when the government set aside $5,000 to purchase and house books that legislators might need to consult. This small collection was housed in the Capitol but was destroyed in 1814 when the British burned the city. Thomas Jefferson, then in retirement at Monticello, offered his personal library as a replacement, noting that "there is, in fact, no subject to which a Member of Congress may not have occasion to refer." Jefferson's collection of 6,487 books, for which Congress eventually paid him $23,950, laid the foundation for the great national library.

By the late 1800s it was clear the Capitol could no longer contain the growing library, and in 1897, the green-domed **Thomas Jefferson Building** was completed. With busts of Dante, Goethe, Hawthorne, and other great writers perched above its entryway, it is certainly decorative. *The Court of*

Neptune, Roland Hinton Perry's fountain at the base of the front steps, rivals some of Rome's best fountains. The **Adams Building,** on 2nd Street behind the Jefferson, was added in 1939. A third structure, the **James Madison Building,** opened in 1980; it is just south of the Jefferson Building, between Independence Avenue and C Street.

In 1997 the Jefferson Building, which had been closed for renovations, was reopened to the public. The gem of the Jefferson Building is the richly decorated Great Hall, adorned with mosaics, paintings, and curving marble stairways. Family trees are explored in the Local History and Genealogy Reading Room. In the Folklife Reading Room, patrons can listen to LP recordings of American Indian music or hear the story of B'rer Rabbit read in the Gullah dialect of Georgia and South Carolina. Items from the library's collection—which includes a Gutenberg Bible—are on display in the Jefferson Building's second-floor Southwest Gallery and Pavilion. ⊠ *Jefferson Bldg., 1st St. and Independence Ave. SE,* ☎ *202/707–8000 taped exhibit information, 202/707–5000 Library of Congress operator, or 202/707–6400 taped schedule of general and special reading-room hours.* 🖵 *Free.* ☾ *Mon.–Sat. 10–5. Tours Mon.–Sat. at 11:30, 1, 2:30, and 4 from Great Hall. Metro: Capitol South.*

❷ National Postal Museum. In the newest member of the Smithsonian family of museums, exhibits underscore the important part the mail played in the development of America and include horse-drawn mail coaches, railway mail cars, airmail planes, every U.S. stamp issued, many foreign stamps, and a collection of philatelic rarities. The National Museum of Natural History may have the Hope Diamond, but the National Postal Museum has the container used to mail the priceless gem to the Smithsonian. The museum takes up only a portion of what is the Washington **City Post Office,** designed by Daniel Burnham and completed in 1914. Nostalgic odes to the noble mail carrier are inscribed on the exterior of the marble building; one of them eulogizes the "Messenger of sympathy and love, servant of parted friends, consoler of the lonely, bond of the scattered family, enlarger of the common life." ⊠ *2 Massachusetts Ave. NE,* ☎ *202/357–2700.* 🖵 *Free.* ☾ *Daily 10–5:30. Metro: Union Station.*

⑤ Peace Monument. A white-marble memorial depicts America in the form of a woman grief-stricken over sailors lost at sea during the Civil War; she is weeping on the shoulder of a second female figure representing History. The plaque inscription refers movingly to navy personnel who "fell in defense of the union and liberty of their country 1861-1865." ⊠ *Traffic circle at 1st St. and Pennsylvania Ave. Metro: Union Station.*

⑬ Sewall-Belmont House. This house, the oldest home on Capitol Hill, is now the headquarters of the National Woman's Party. Its museum chronicles the early days of the women's movement and is filled with period furniture and portraits and busts of such suffrage-movement leaders as Lucretia Mott, Elizabeth Cady Stanton, and Alice Paul. The redbrick house was built in 1800 by Robert Sewall. From 1801 to 1813 Secretary of the Treasury Albert Gallatin, who finalized the details of the Louisiana Purchase in his front-parlor office, lived here. ⊠ *144 Constitution Ave. NE,* ☎ *202/546-3989.* ⊠ *Free.* ☽ *Tues.–Fri. 10–3, Sat. noon–4. Metro: Union Station.*

⑫ Supreme Court Building. It wasn't until 1935 that the Supreme Court got its own building: a white-marble temple with twin rows of Corinthian columns designed by Cass Gilbert. In 1800, the justices arrived in Washington along with the rest of the government but were for years shunted around various rooms in the Capitol; for a while they even met in a tavern. William Howard Taft, the only man to serve as both president and chief justice, was instrumental in getting the court a home of its own, though he died before it was completed.

The Supreme Court convenes on the first Monday in October and remains in session until it has heard all of its cases and handed down all its decisions (usually the end of June). On Monday through Wednesday of two weeks in each month, the justices hear oral arguments in the velvet-swathed court chamber. Visitors who want to listen can choose to wait in either of two lines. One, the "three-to-five-minute" line, shuttles visitors through, giving them a quick impression of the court at work. The other is for those who'd like to stay for the whole show; it's best to be in line by 8:30 AM. ⊠ *1st and E. Capitol Sts. NE,* ☎ *202/479–3000.* ☎ *Free.* ⊙ *Weekdays 9–4:30. Metro: Capitol South.*

❸ Thurgood Marshall Federal Judiciary Building. If you're in the Union Station neighborhood, the signature work of architect Edward Larabee Barnes is worth taking a moment to pop inside for a look at its spectacular atrium with a garden of bamboo five stories tall. ⊠ *Massachusetts Ave. opposite Union Station. Metro: Union Station.*

❶ Union Station. In 1902 the McMillan Commission—charged with suggesting ways to improve the appearance of the city—recommended that the many train lines that sliced through the capital share one main depot. Union Station was opened in 1908 and was the first building completed under the commission's plan. Chicago architect and commission member Daniel H. Burnham patterned the station after the Roman Baths of Diocletian.

The Union Station you see today is the result of a restoration completed in 1988, an effort intended to be the beginning of a revival of Washington's east end. The jewel of the structure remains its meticulously restored main waiting room. Forty-six statues of Roman legionnaires, one for each state in the Union when the station was completed, ring the grand room. The east hall, now filled with vendors, was once an expensive restaurant. The **Columbus Memorial Fountain,** designed by Lorado Taft, sits in the plaza in front of Union Station. A caped, steely-eyed Christopher Columbus stares into the distance, flanked by a hoary, bearded figure (the Old World) and an Indian brave (the New). ⊠ *Massachusetts Ave. north of Capitol,* ☎ *202/289–1908. Metro: Union Station.*

❽ United States Botanic Garden. The rather cold exterior belies the peaceful, plant-filled oasis within. The conservatory includes a cactus house, a fern house, and a subtropical house filled with orchids. Seasonal displays include blooming plants at Easter, chrysanthemums in the fall, and Christmas greens and poinsettias in December and January. Brochures just inside the doorway offer helpful gardening tips. ⊠ *1st St. and Maryland Ave. SW,* ☎ *202/225–8333.* ☎ *Free.* ⊙ *Daily 9–5. Metro: Federal Center SW.*

Old Downtown and Federal Triangle

Nowhere have the city's imperfections been more visible than on L'Enfant's grand thoroughfare, Pennsylvania Avenue. By the early '60s it had become a national disgrace, the dilapidated buildings that lined it home to pawn shops and cheap souvenir stores. While riding up Pennsylvania Avenue in his inaugural parade, a disgusted John F. Kennedy is said to have turned to an aide and said, "Fix it!" Washington's downtown—once within the diamond formed by Massachusetts, Louisiana, Pennsylvania, and New York avenues—had its problems, too, many as a result of the riots that rocked the capital in 1968 after the assassination of Martin Luther King Jr. In their wake, many downtown businesses left the area and moved north of the White House. In recent years developers have rediscovered "old downtown," and buildings are now being torn down or remodeled at an amazing pace. After several false starts Pennsylvania Avenue is shining once again.

Numbers in the margin correspond to points of interest on the Old Downtown and Federal Triangle map.

Sights to See

❺ Ford's Theatre. In 1861, Baltimore theater impresario John T. Ford leased the First Baptist Church building that stood on this site and turned it into a successful music hall. The building burned down late in 1862, and Ford rebuilt it. The events of April 14, 1865, would shock the nation and close the theater. On that night, during a production of *Our American Cousin,* John Wilkes Booth entered the presidential box and assassinated Abraham Lincoln. The stricken president was carried across the street to the house of tailor William Petersen. Charles Augustus Leale, a 23-year-old doctor, attended to the president, whose injuries would have left him blind had he ever regained consciousness. To let Lincoln know that someone was nearby, Leale held his hand throughout the night. Lincoln died the next morning.

The federal government bought Ford's Theatre in 1866 for $100,000 and converted it into office space. It was remodeled as a Lincoln museum in 1932 and was restored to its 1865 appearance in 1968. The basement museum—with artifacts such as Booth's pistol and the clothes Lincoln was

Old Downtown and Federal Triangle

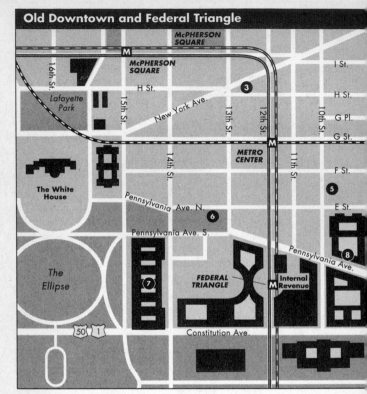

Ford's
Theatre, **5**

Freedom
Plaza, **6**

Friendship
Arch, **2**

J. Edgar
Hoover FBI
Building, **8**

National
Aquarium, **7**

National
Archives, **9**

National
Museum of
Women in the
Arts, **3**

Old Patent
Office Building/
National
Museum of
American Art
and National
Portrait
Gallery, **4**

Pension
Building/
National
Building
Museum, **1**

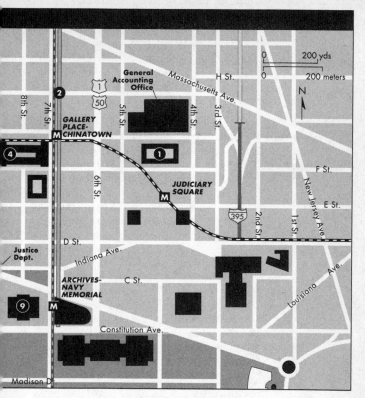

General Accounting Office

Massachusetts Ave.

H St.

200 yds

200 meters

N

8th St.

7th St.

GALLERY PLACE-CHINATOWN

5th St.

4th St.

3rd St.

1

JUDICIARY SQUARE

F St.

E St.

6th St.

New Jersey Ave.

395

2nd St.

1st St.

Justice Dept.

D St.

Indiana Ave.

ARCHIVES-NAVY MEMORIAL

C St.

Louisiana Ave.

Constitution Ave.

Madison D

wearing when he was shot—reopened in 1990. The theater itself continues to present a complete schedule of plays. *A Christmas Carol* is an annual holiday favorite. ⊠ *511 10th St. NW,* ☎ *202/426–6924.* 🎫 *Free.* ⊘ *Daily 9–5; theater closed when rehearsals or matinees are in progress (generally Thurs. and weekends); Lincoln Museum in basement remains open at these times. Metro: Metro Center.*

❻ Freedom Plaza. In 1988 Western Plaza was renamed Freedom Plaza in honor of Dr. Martin Luther King. Freedom Plaza's east end is dominated by a **statue of General Casimir Pułaski,** the Polish nobleman who led an American cavalry corps during the Revolutionary War and was mortally wounded in 1779 at the Siege of Savannah. He gazes over a plaza that is inlaid in bronze with a detail from L'Enfant's original 1791 plan for the Federal City. Bronze outlines the President's Palace and the Congress House; the Mall is represented by a green lawn. Cut into the edges are quotations about the capital city, not all of them complimentary. To compare L'Enfant's vision with today's reality, stand in the middle of the map's Pennsylvania Avenue and look west. L'Enfant had planned an unbroken vista from the Capitol to the White House, but the Treasury Building, begun in 1836, ruined the view. ⊠ *Bounded by 13th, 14th, and E Sts. and Pennsylvania Ave. Metro: Federal Triangle.*

❷ Friendship Arch. A colorful and ornate 75-ft-wide arch is a reminder of Washington's sister-city relationship with Beijing. ⊠ *Spanning H Street at 7th Street. Metro: Gallery Place/Chinatown.*

⟳ ❽ J. Edgar Hoover Federal Bureau of Investigation Building. The one-hour tour of the FBI building remains one of the most popular tourist activities in the city. A brief film outlines the Bureau's work, while exhibits describe famous past cases and illustrate the FBI's fight against organized crime, terrorism, bank robbery, espionage, extortion, and other criminal activities. There's everything from gangster John Dillinger's death mask to a poster display of the 10 Most Wanted criminals. You'll also see the laboratories where the FBI painstakingly studies evidence. At the end of the tour, a special agent gives a live-ammo firearms demonstration in the building's indoor shooting range. ⊠ *10th St. and Pennsylvania Ave. NW, tour entrance on E St. NW,* ☏ *202/324–3447.* 🎫 *Free.* ☼ *Tours weekdays 8:45–4:15. Metro: Federal Triangle.*

🖐 **❼ National Aquarium.** The western base of Federal Triangle between 14th and 15th streets is the home of the Department of Commerce, charged with promoting U.S. economic development and technological advancement. It's a good thing there's plenty of space; incongruously, the National Aquarium is housed inside. Established in 1873, it's the country's oldest public aquarium, with more than 1,200 fish and other creatures representing 250 species of fresh- and saltwater life on display. Its tanks are alive with brilliantly colored tropical fish from every corner of the globe, firehose-thick moray eels, frogs and turtles, piranhas, and sharks. A "touch tank" lets you handle more hospitable sea creatures such as crabs and oysters. ⊠ *14th St. and Pennsylvania Ave. NW,* ☏ *202/482–2825.* 🎫 *$2.* ☼ *Daily 9–5; sharks fed Mon., Wed., and Sat. at 2; piranhas fed Tues., Thurs., and Sun. at 2. Metro: Federal Triangle.*

❾ National Archives. If the Smithsonian Institution is the nation's attic, the Archives is the nation's basement, and it bears responsibility for the cataloguing and safekeeping of important government documents and other items. The Declaration of Independence, the Constitution, and the Bill of Rights are on display in the Rotunda. Other objects in the Archives' vast collection include bureaucratic correspondence, veterans and immigration records, treaties, and even Richard Nixon's resignation letter and the rifle Lee Harvey Oswald used to assassinate John F. Kennedy. ⊠ *Constitution Ave. between 7th and 9th Sts. NW,* ☏ *202/501–5000.* 🎫 *Free.* ☼ *Apr.–Labor Day, daily 10–9; Sept.–Mar., daily 10–5:30; tour weekdays at 10:15 and 1:15. Metro: Archives/Navy Memorial.*

National Museum of American Art. The first floor of the National Museum of American Art, which is in the ☞ **Old Patent Office Building,** holds displays of early American art and art of the West, as well as a gallery of painted miniatures. On the second floor are works by the American Impressionists, including John Henry Twachtman and Childe

Hassam. There are also plaster models and marble sculptures by Hiram Powers, including the plaster cast of his famous work *The Greek Slave,* the original of which is housed in the Corcoran Gallery (☞ The White House Area, *above*). Just outside the room containing Powers's work is a copy of a sculpture Augustus Saint-Gaudens created for Henry Adams. Adams's wife had committed suicide and the original of this moving, shroud-draped figure sits above her grave in Rock Creek Cemetery. Also on this floor are massive landscapes by Albert Bierstadt and Thomas Moran. The third floor is filled with modern art, including works by Leon Kroll and Edward Hopper that were commissioned during the '30s by the federal government. The Lincoln Gallery—site of the receiving line at Abraham Lincoln's 1865 inaugural ball—has been restored to its original appearance and contains modern art by Jasper Johns, Robert Rauschenberg, Milton Avery, Kenneth Noland, and others. ✉ *8th and G Sts. NW,* ☎ *202/357–2700, TTY 202/357–1729.* 🎫 *Free.* ☉ *Daily 10–5:30. Metro: Gallery Place.*

❸ **National Museum of Women in the Arts.** Works by prominent female artists from the Renaissance to the present are showcased in this beautifully restored 1907 Renaissance Revival building, one of the larger non-Smithsonian museums, designed by Waddy Wood. Ironically, it was once a men-only Masonic temple. In addition to displaying traveling shows, the museum houses a permanent collection that includes paintings, drawings, sculpture, prints, and photographs by such artists as Georgia O'Keeffe, Mary Cassatt, Élisabeth Vigée-Lebrun, Frida Kahlo, and Judy Chicago. ✉ *1250 New York Ave. NW,* ☎ *202/783–5000.* 🎫 *Suggested donation $3.* ☉ *Mon.–Sat. 10–5, Sun. noon–5. Metro: Metro Center.*

National Portrait Gallery. This museum is in the ☞ Old Patent Office Building along with the ☞ National Museum of American Art. The best place to start a circuit of the Portrait Gallery is on the restored third floor. The mezzanine level of the wonderfully busy room features a Civil War exhibition, with portraits, photographs, and lithographs of such wartime personalities as Julia Ward Howe, Frederick Douglass, Ulysses S. Grant, and Robert E. Lee. There are also life casts of Abraham Lincoln's hands and face. The

Renaissance-style gallery has been restored to its original splendor, complete with colorful tile flooring and a stained-glass skylight. Highlights of the Portrait Gallery's second floor include the **Hall of Presidents** (featuring a portrait or sculpture of each chief executive) and the George Washington "Lansdowne" portrait. The first floor features portraits of well-known American athletes and performers. *Time* magazine gave the museum its collection of Person of the Year covers and many other photos and paintings that the magazine has commissioned over the years. Parts of this collection are periodically on display. ⊠ *8th and F Sts. NW,* ☎ *202/357–2700, TTY 202/357–1729.* ✆ *Free.* ☉ *Daily 10–5:30. Metro: Gallery Place.*

❹ **Old Patent Office Building.** Two Smithsonian museums now share the Old Patent Office Building. The ☞ **National Portrait Gallery** is on the south side; the ☞ **National Museum of American Art** is to the north. Construction on the south wing, which was designed by Washington Monument architect Robert Mills, started in 1836. When the huge Greek-Revival quadrangle was completed in 1867 it was the largest building in the country. Many of its rooms housed glass display cabinets filled with the models that inventors were required to submit with their patent applications. During the Civil War, the Patent Office, like many other buildings in the city, was turned into a hospital. Among those caring for the wounded here were Clara Barton and Walt Whitman. The Smithsonian opened it to the public in 1968. ⊠ *G St. between 7th and 9th Sts.*

❶ **Pension Building.** The open interior of this mammoth red-brick edifice is one of the city's great spaces and has been the site of inaugural balls for more than 100 years. The eight central Corinthian columns are the largest in the world, rising to a height of 75 ft. Though they look like marble, each is made of 75,000 bricks, covered with plaster and painted to resemble Siena marble. The building was erected between 1882 and 1887 to house workers who processed the pension claims of veterans and their survivors. The architect was U.S. Army Corps of Engineers General Montgomery C. Meigs, who took as his inspiration the Italian Renaissance–style Palazzo Farnese in Rome. The Pension Building now houses the **National Building Museum,** devoted to architecture and the building arts. "Washington: Symbol and City" is a permanent exhibit that outlines the capital's architectural history, from monumental core to residential neighborhoods. Recent temporary exhibits have explored the rebuilding of Oklahoma City and the dome as a symbol of American democracy. ⊠ *F St. between 4th and 5th Sts. NW,* ☎ *202/272–2448.* ⊠ *Free.* ⊙ *Mon.– Sat. 10–4, Sun. noon–4; tour weekdays at 12:30, weekends at 12:30 and 1:30. Metro: Judiciary Square.*

Georgetown

The area that would come to be known as George (after George II), then George Towne and, finally, Georgetown, was part of Maryland when it was settled in the early 1700s by Scottish immigrants. Georgetown's position at the farthest point up the Potomac accessible by boat made it an ideal transit-and-inspection point for farmers who grew tobacco in Maryland's interior. In 1789 the state granted the town a charter, but two years later Georgetown—along with Alexandria, its counterpart in Virginia—was included by George Washington in the Territory of Columbia, site of the new capital.

Tobacco eventually became a less important commodity, and Georgetown became a milling center, using water power from the Potomac. When the Chesapeake & Ohio (C&O) Canal was completed in 1850, the city intensified its milling operations and became the eastern end of a waterway that stretched 184 mi to the west. The canal took up some of the slack when Georgetown's harbor began to fill with silt and the port lost business to Alexandria and Baltimore, but never became the success it was meant to be. In the years that followed, Georgetown was a far cry from the fashionable spot it is today. Clustered near the water were a foundry, a fish market, paper and cotton mills, and a power station for the city's streetcar system. It still had its Georgian, Federal, and Victorian homes, though, and when the New Deal and World War II brought a flood of newcomers to Washington, Georgetown's tree-shaded streets and handsome brick houses were rediscovered.

Washington has filled in around Georgetown over the years, but the former tobacco port retains an air of aloofness. It's narrow streets, which refuse to conform to Pierre L'Enfant's plan for the Federal City, make up the Capital's wealthiest neighborhood and are the nucleus of its nightlife. Its lack of a Metro station means you'll have to take a bus or walk to Georgetown. It's about a 15-minute walk from the Dupont Circle or Foggy Bottom Metro station. (If you'd rather take a bus, the G2 Georgetown University bus goes from Dupont Circle west along P Street. The 34 and 36 Friendship Heights buses leave from 22nd and Pennsylvania and deposit you at 31st and M.)

Numbers in the margin correspond to points of interest on the Georgetown map.

Sights to See

♻ **C&O Canal.** This waterway kept Georgetown open to shipping after its harbor had filled with silt. George Washington was one of the first to advance the idea of a canal linking the Potomac with the Ohio River across the Appalachians. Work started on the C&O Canal in 1828, and when it opened in 1850, its 74 locks linked Georgetown with Cumberland, Maryland. Lumber, coal, iron, wheat, and flour moved up and down the canal, but it was never as successful as its planners had hoped it would be. Many of the bridges spanning the canal in Georgetown were too low to allow anything other than fully loaded barges to pass underneath, and competition from the Baltimore & Ohio Railroad eventually spelled an end to profitability. Today the canal is a part of the National Park system, and walkers follow the towpath once used by mules while canoeists paddle the canal's calm waters. ⊠ *1057 Thomas Jefferson St. NW,* ☎ *202/653–5190;* ⊠ *Great Falls* ☎ *301/299–3613.* ▣ *$6.* ☉ *90-min barge trip mid-Apr.–early Nov., Wed.– Sun. at 11, 1, and 3.*

❸ **Cox's Row.** Architecture buffs, especially those interested in Federal and Victorian houses, enjoy wandering along the redbrick sidewalks of upper Georgetown. To get a representative taste of the houses in the area, walk along the 3300 block of N Street. The group of five Federal houses between 3339 and 3327 N Street is known collectively as Cox's Row, after John Cox, a former mayor of Georgetown, who built

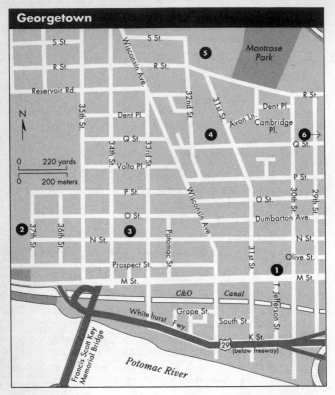

Georgetown

them in 1817. The flat-front, redbrick Federal house at 3307 N Street was the home of then-Senator John F. Kennedy and his family before the White House beckoned.

⑥ Dumbarton House. Its symmetry and the two curved wings on the north side make Dumbarton, built around 1800, a distinctive example of Georgian architecture. Eight rooms inside Dumbarton House have been restored to Colonial splendor, with period furnishings such as mahogany American Chippendale chairs, hallmark silver, Persian rugs, and a breakfront cabinet filled with rare books. Other notable items include a 1789 Charles Willson Peale portrait of Benjamin Stoddert's children (with an early view of Georgetown harbor in the background), Martha Washington's traveling cloak, and a British redcoat's red coat. ⊠ *2715 Q St. NW,* ☎ *202/337–2288.* ☞ *Suggested donation $3.* ⊙ *Tues.–Sat. 10–12:15.*

⑤ Dumbarton Oaks. In 1944 one of the most important events of the 20th century took place in Dumbarton Oaks, when representatives of the United States, Great Britain, China, and the Soviet Union met in the music room here to lay the groundwork for the United Nations.

Career diplomat Robert Woods Bliss and his wife Mildred bought the property in 1920 and set about removing the 19th-century additions that had marred the Federal lines of the 1801 mansion. In 1940 the Blisses conveyed the estate to Harvard University, which maintains world-renowned collections of Byzantine and pre-Columbian art there. The Byzantine collection includes beautiful examples of both religious and secular items executed in mosaic, metal, enamel, and ivory. Pre-Columbian works—artifacts and textiles from Mexico and Central and South America by such peoples as the Aztec, Maya, and Olmec—are arranged in an enclosed glass pavilion designed by Philip Johnson. Dumbarton Oaks's 10 acres of formal gardens is one of the loveliest spots in all of Washington. Designed by noted landscape architect Beatrix Farrand, the gardens incorporate elements of traditional English, Italian, and French styles. Plenty of well-positioned benches make this a good place for resting weary feet, too. ⊠ *Art collections, 1703 32nd St. NW,* ☎ *202/339–6401 or 202/339–6400;* ⊠ *Gardens, 31st and*

R Sts. NW. 🎫 *Art collections, suggested donation $1; gardens Apr.–Oct. $3, Nov.–Mar. free.* ⏲ *Art collections Tues.–Sun. 2–5; gardens Apr.–Oct., daily 2–6; Nov.–Mar., daily 2–5.*

❷ **Georgetown University.** Founded in 1789 by John Carroll, first American bishop and first archbishop of Baltimore, Georgetown is the oldest Jesuit school in the country. About 12,000 students attend Georgetown, known now as much for its perennially successful basketball team as for its fine programs in law, medicine, foreign service, and the liberal arts. When seen from the Potomac or from Washington's high ground, the Gothic spires of Georgetown's older buildings give the university an almost medieval look. ✉ *37th and O Sts.,* ☎ *202/687–5055.*

❶ **Old Stone House.** What was early American life like? Here's the capital's oldest window into the past. Work on this fieldstone house, thought to be Washington's only surviving pre-Revolutionary building, was begun in 1764 by a cabinetmaker named Christopher Layman. The house, now a museum, was used as both a residence and a place of business by a succession of occupants. Five of the house's rooms are furnished with the simple sturdy artifacts—plain tables, spinning wheels, etc.—of 18th-century middle-class life. The National Park Service maintains the house and its lovely gardens in the rear, which are planted with fruit trees and perennials. ✉ *3051 M St. NW,* ☎ *202/426–6851.* 🎫 *Free.* ⏲ *Memorial Day–Labor Day, daily 9–5; Labor Day–Memorial Day, Wed.–Sun. 9–5.*

❹ **Tudor Place.** Stop at Q Street between 31st and 32nd streets, look through the trees to the north, at the top of a sloping lawn, and you'll see the neoclassic Tudor Place, designed by Capitol architect William Thornton and completed in 1816. On a house tour you'll see chairs that belonged to George Washington and Francis Scott Key's desk. The grounds contain many specimens planted in the early 19th century. The house was built for Thomas Peter, son of Georgetown's first mayor, and his wife, Martha Custis, Martha Washington's granddaughter. It was because of this connection to the president's family that Tudor Place came to house many items from Mount Vernon. Tour reser-

vations are advised. ✉ *1644 31st St. NW,* ☎ *202/965–0400.*
💳 *Suggested donation $6.* ⏱ *Tour Tues.–Fri. at 10, 11:30,
1, and 2:30; Sat. hourly 10–4 (last tour at 3); garden spring
and fall, Sun. noon–4.*

Dupont Circle

Originally known as Pacific Circle, this hub was the west-
ernmost circle in Pierre L'Enfant's original design for the
Federal City. The name was changed in 1884, when Congress
authorized construction of a bronze statue honoring Civil
War hero Admiral Samuel F. Dupont. The statue fell into
disrepair, and Dupont's family—who had never liked it anyway—replaced it in 1921 with the fountain you see today.
The marble fountain, with its allegorical figures Sea, Stars,
and Wind, was created by Daniel Chester French, the sculptor of Lincoln's statue in the Lincoln Memorial. Since a half-
dozen streets converge on Dupont Circle, the buildings
around it are, for the most part, wedge shaped and set on
oddly cut plots of land like massive slices of pie.

Dupont Circle is more than a deserted island around which
traffic flows, making it an exception among Washington
circles. The activity on the circle spills over into the surrounding streets, one of the liveliest, most vibrant neighborhoods in Washington, with many restaurants, offbeat
shops, and specialty bookstores. Stores and clubs catering
to the neighborhood's large gay community are abundant.

*Numbers in the margin correspond to points of interest on
the Dupont Circle and Foggy Bottom map.*

Sights to See

❷ Anderson House. Larz Anderson was a diplomat whose career included postings to Japan and Belgium. Anderson and
his heiress wife, Isabel, toured the world, picking up objects that struck their fancy. They filled their residence,
which was constructed in 1905, with the booty of their trav-
els, including choir stalls from an Italian Renaissance
church, Flemish tapestries, and a large—if spotty—collection of Asian art. All this remains on display in the house.

In accordance with Anderson's wishes, the building also
serves as the headquarters of a group to which he belonged:

Dupont Circle and Foggy Bottom

KEY

 American Express Office

Anderson
House, **2**

Bison Bridge, **3**

B'nai B'rith
Klutznick
Museum, **9**

Council
House, **10**

Department
of State
Building, **15**

Federal
Reserve
Building, **16**

George
Washington
University, **13**

Heurich
Mansion/
Historical
Society of
Washington,
D.C., **1**

Metropolitan
African
Methodist
Episcopal
Church, **11**

National
Geographic
Society, **12**

National
Museum of
American
Jewish Military
History, **7**

Phillips
Collection, **6**

St. Matthew's
Cathedral, **8**

Textile
Museum, **5**

Watergate, **14**

Woodrow
Wilson
House, **4**

the **Society of the Cincinnati.** The oldest patriotic organization in the country, the society was formed in 1783 by a group of officers who had served with George Washington during the Revolutionary War. The group took the name Cincinnati from Cincinnatus, a distinguished Roman who, circa 500 BC, led an army against Rome's enemies and later quelled civil disturbances in the city. After each success, rather than seek political power that could have easily been his, he returned to the idealistic purity of a simple life on his farm. The story impressed the American officers, who saw in it a mirror of their own situation: They too would leave the battlefields behind to get on with the business of forging a new nation. (One such member went on to name the city in Ohio.) Today's members are direct descendants of those American revolutionaries.

Many of the displays in the society's museum focus on the Colonial period and the Revolutionary War. One room—painted in a marvelous trompe l'oeil style—is filled with military miniatures from the United States and France. (Because of the important role France played in defeating the British, French officers were invited to join the society. Pierre L'Enfant, "Artist of the Revolution" and planner of Washington, designed the society's eagle medallion.) Amid the glitz, glamour, beauty, and patriotic spectacle of the mansion are two delightful painted panels in the solarium that depict the Andersons' favorite motor-car sightseeing routes around Washington. ⊠ *2118 Massachusetts Ave. NW,* ☎ *202/785–2040.* 🖼 *Free.* ☉ *Tues.–Sat. 1–4. Metro: Dupont Circle.*

❸ **Bison Bridge.** Tour guides at the Smithsonian's Museum of Natural History are quick to remind visitors that America never had buffalo; the big shaggy animals that roamed the plains were bison. Though many maps and guidebooks call this the Buffalo Bridge, the four bronze statues by A. Phimister Proctor are of bison. Officially called the **Dumbarton Bridge,** the structure stretches across Rock Creek Park into Georgetown. Its sides are decorated with busts of Native Americans, the work of architect Glenn Brown, who, along with his son Bedford, designed the bridge in 1914. The best way to see the busts is to walk the footpath along Rock Creek. ⊠ *23rd and Q Sts. NW. Metro: Dupont Circle.*

9 **B'nai B'rith Klutznick Museum.** Devoted to the history of Jewish people, this museum's permanent exhibits span 20 centuries and highlight Jewish festivals and the rituals employed to mark the various stages of life. A wide variety of Jewish decorative art, adorning such items as spice boxes and Torah covers, is on display. Changing exhibits highlight the work of contemporary Jewish artists. ⊠ *1640 Rhode Island Ave. NW,* ☎ *202/857–6583.* 🎫 *Suggested donation $2.* ☉ *Sun.–Fri. 10–5. Metro: Dupont Circle or Farragut North.*

10 **Council House.** Exhibits in this museum focus on the achievements of black women, including Mary McLeod Bethune, who founded Florida's Bethune-Cookman College, established the National Council of Negro Women, and served as an adviser to President Franklin D. Roosevelt. The nearest sight is Scott Circle. ⊠ *1318 Vermont Ave. NW,* ☎ *202/ 673–2402.* 🎫 *Free.* ☉ *Mon.–Sat. 10–4. Metro: McPherson Square.*

1 **Heurich Mansion.** Currently housing the **Historical Society of Washington, D.C.,** the Heurich Mansion is a severe Romanesque Revival building that was the home of Christian Heurich, a German orphan who made his fortune in this country in the beer business. Heurich's brewery was in the Foggy Bottom neighborhood, where the Kennedy Center stands today. After Heurich's widow died, in 1955, the house was turned over to the Historical Society and today is its headquarters and houses its voluminous archives. All the furnishings in the house were owned and used by the Heurichs. The interior of the house is an eclectic Victorian treasure trove of plaster detailing, carved wooden doors, and painted ceilings. Guides who give tours of the house are adept at answering questions about other Washington landmarks, too. ⊠ *1307 New Hampshire Ave. NW,* ☎ *202/785–2068.* 🎫 *$3.* ☉ *Wed.–Sat. 10–4. Metro: Dupont Circle.*

11 **Metropolitan African Methodist Episcopal Church.** Completed in 1886, the Gothic-style Metropolitan African Methodist Episcopal Church became one of the most influential black churches in the city. Abolitionist orator Frederick Douglass worshiped here, and Bill Clinton chose the church as the setting for his inaugural prayer service.

✉ *1518 M St. NW,* ☎ *202/331–1426. Metro: Farragut North.*

🐾 ⓬ **National Geographic Society.** Founded in 1888, the society is best known for its yellow-border magazine, found in doctor's offices, family rooms, and attics across the country. The society has sponsored numerous expeditions throughout its 100-year history, including those of Admirals Peary and Byrd and underwater explorer Jacques Cousteau. At **Explorers Hall,** you can experience everything from a minitornado to video "touch-screens" that explain various geographic concepts and then quiz you on what you've learned. The most dramatic events take place in Earth Station One, a 72-seat amphitheater that sends the audience on a journey around the world. The centerpiece is a hand-painted globe, 11 ft in diameter, that floats and spins on a cushion of air, showing off different features of the planet. ✉ *17th and M Sts.,* ☎ *202/857–7588; group tours, 202/857–7689.* ▣ *Free.* ☉ *Mon.–Sat. and holidays 9–5, Sun. 10–5. Metro: Farragut North.*

❼ **National Museum of American Jewish Military History.** The museum's focus is on American Jews who have served in every war the nation has fought. On display are their weapons, uniforms, medals, recruitment posters, and other military memorabilia. The few specifically religious items— a camouflage yarmulke, rabbinical supplies fashioned from shell casings and parachute silk—underscore the strange demands placed on religion during war. ✉ *1811 R St. NW,* ☎ *202/265–6280.* ▣ *Free.* ☉ *Weekdays 9–5, Sun. 1–5. Metro: Dupont Circle.*

❻ **Phillips Collection.** The first permanent museum of modern art in the country, the masterpiece-filled Phillips Collection is unique both in origin and content. In 1918 Duncan Phillips, grandson of a founder of the Jones and Laughlin Steel Company, started to collect art for a museum that would stand as a memorial to his father and brother, who had died within 13 months of each other. Three years later what was first called the Phillips Memorial Gallery opened in two rooms of this Georgian-Revival home near Dupont Circle. Holdings include works by Georges Braque, Paul Cézanne, Paul Klee, Henri Matisse, John Henry Twachtman, and the largest museum collection in the country of the work of Pierre Bonnard. The exhibits change regularly. The collection's best-known paintings include Renoir's *Luncheon of the Boating Party, Repentant Peter* by both Goya and El Greco, *A Bowl of Plums* by 18th-century artist Jean-Baptiste Siméon Chardin, Degas's *Dancers at the Bar,* Van Gogh's *Entrance to the Public Garden at Arles,* and Cézanne's self-portrait, the painting Phillips said he would save first if his gallery caught fire. During the '20s, Phillips and his wife, Marjorie, started to support American Modernists such as John Marin, Georgia O'Keeffe, and Arthur Dove.

The Phillips is a comfortable museum. Works of a favorite artist are often grouped together in "exhibition units," and, unlike most other galleries (where uniformed guards appear uninterested in the masterpieces around them), the Phillips employs students of art, many of whom are artists themselves, to sit by the paintings and answer questions. ⊠ *1600 21st St. NW,* ☎ *202/387–2151.* 🎫 *$6.50, Thurs. night $5.* ⊘ *Tues., Wed., Fri., and Sat. 10–5; Thurs. 10–8:30; Sun. noon–7 (noon–5 June–Aug.); tour Wed. and Sat. at 2; gallery talks 1st and 3rd Thurs. of month at 12:30. Metro: Dupont Circle.*

8 St. Matthew's Cathedral. St. Matthew's is the seat of Washington's Catholic archbishop. John F. Kennedy frequently worshiped in this Renaissance-style church, and in 1963 his funeral mass was held within its richly decorated walls. Set in the floor, directly in front of the main altar, is a memorial to the slain president: "Here rested the remains of President Kennedy at the requiem mass November 25, 1963, before their removal to Arlington where they lie in expectation of a heavenly resurrection." ⊠ *1725 Rhode Island Ave. NW,* ☎ *202/347–3215.* 🎫 *Free.* ⊘ *Weekdays and Sun. 7–6:30, Sat. 7:30–6:30; tour usually Sun. at 2:30. Metro: Farragut North.*

5 Textile Museum. In the 1890s, founder George Hewitt Myers purchased his first Oriental rug for his dorm room at Yale and subsequently collected more than 12,000 textiles and 1,500 carpets. An heir to the Bristol-Myers fortune, Myers and his wife lived two houses down from

Woodrow Wilson, at 2310 S Street, in a home designed by John Russell Pope, architect of the National Archives and Jefferson Memorial. Myers bought the Waddy Wood–designed house next door, at Number 2320, and opened his museum to the public in 1925. Rotating exhibits are taken from a permanent collection of historic and ethnographic items that include Coptic and pre-Columbian textiles, Kashmir embroidery, and Turkman tribal rugs. At least one show of modern textiles—such as quilts or fiber art—is mounted each year. ⊠ *2320 S St. NW,* ☎ *202/667–0441.* ⌨ *Suggested donation $5.* ☉ *Mon.–Sat. 10–5, Sun. 1–5; highlight tour Sept.–May, Wed. and weekends at 2. Metro: Dupont Circle.*

❹ **Woodrow Wilson House.** Wilson is the only president who stayed in Washington after leaving the White House. (He's also the only president buried in the city, inside the Washington Cathedral.) He and his second wife, Edith Bolling Wilson, retired in 1920 to this Georgian Revival house designed by Washington architect Waddy B. Wood. (Wood also designed the Department of the Interior Building and the National Museum of Women in the Arts building.) The house was built in 1915 for a carpet magnate.

President Wilson suffered a stroke toward the end of his second term, in 1919, and he lived out the last few years of his life on this quiet street. He died in 1924. Edith survived him by 37 years. After she died in 1961, the house and its contents were bequeathed to the National Trust for Historic Preservation. On view are such items as a Gobelins tapestry, a baseball signed by King George V, and the shell casing from the first shot fired by U.S. forces in World War I. The house also contains memorabilia related to the history of the short-lived League of Nations, including the colorful flag Wilson hoped would be adopted by that organization. ⊠ *2340 S St. NW,* ☎ *202/387–4062.* ⌨ *$5.* ☉ *Tues.–Sun. 10–4. Metro: Dupont Circle.*

Foggy Bottom

The Foggy Bottom area of Washington—bordered roughly by the Potomac and Rock Creek to the west, 20th Street to the east, Pennsylvania Avenue to the north, and Constitution Avenue to the south—has three main claims to fame: the State Department, the Kennedy Center, and George Washington University. In 1763 a German immigrant named Jacob Funk purchased this land, and a community called Funkstown sprang up on the Potomac. This nickname is only slightly less amusing than the present one, an appellation that is derived from the wharves, breweries, lime kilns, and glassworks that were near the water. Smoke from these factories combined with the swampy air of the low-lying ground to produce a permanent fog along the waterfront.

The smoke-belching factories ensured work for the hundreds of German and Irish immigrants who settled in Foggy Bottom in the 19th century. By the 1930s, however, industry was on the way out, and Foggy Bottom had become a poor, predominantly black part of Washington. The opening of the State Department headquarters in 1947 reawakened middle-class interest in the neighborhood's modest row houses. Many of them are now gone, and Foggy Bottom today suffers from a split personality, and tiny, one-room-wide row houses sit next to large, mixed-use developments.

While the Foggy Bottom neighborhood has its own Metro stop, many attractions are a considerable distance away. If you don't relish long walks or time is limited, check the Foggy Bottom map to see if you need to make alternate travel arrangements to visit specific sights.

Numbers in the margin correspond to points of interest on the Dupont Circle and Foggy Bottom map.

Sights to See

⑮ Department of State building. The foreign policy of the United States is formulated and administered by battalions of brainy analysts in the huge Department of State building (often referred to as the State Department), which also serves as the headquarters of the United States Diplomatic Corps. All is presided over by the Secretary of State, who is fourth in line for the presidency (after the Vice President, Speaker of the House, and president *pro tempore* of the Senate) should the president be unable to serve. On the top floor are the opulent **Diplomatic Reception Rooms,** decorated in the manner of great halls of Europe, and the rooms of Colonial American plantations. The museum-quality furnishings include a Philadelphia highboy, a Paul Revere bowl, and the desk on which the Treaty of Paris was signed. You'll need to register for a tour well in advance of your visit. Summer tours must be booked up to three months in advance. ⊠ *23rd and C Sts. NW,* ☎ *202/647–3241, TTY 202/736–4474.* 🖃 *Free.* ☉ *Tour weekdays at 9:30, 10:30, and 2:45. Metro: Foggy Bottom.*

⑯ Federal Reserve Building. Whether or not interest rates are raised or lowered in an attempt to control the economy gets decided in this imposing marble edifice, its bronze entry-way topped by a massive eagle. Designed by Folger Library architect Paul Cret, "the Fed" is on Constitution Avenue between 21st and 20th streets. It seems to say, "Your money's safe with us." Even so, there isn't any money here. Ft. Knox and New York's Federal Reserve Bank hold most of the Federal Reserve System's gold. The stolid building is a bit more human inside, with a varied collection of art and four special art exhibitions every year. A 45-minute tour includes a film that attempts to explain exactly what it is that "the Fed" does. Call 202/452–3149 to arrange a building tour, or 202/452–3686 to arrange an art tour. ⊠ *Enter on C St. between 20th and 21st Sts.,* ☎ *202/452–3000.* 🖃 *Free.* ☉ *Weekdays 11–2, building tour Thurs. at 2:30. Metro: Foggy Bottom.*

⑬ George Washington University. George Washington had always hoped the capital would be home to a world-class university. He even left 50 shares of stock in the Patowmack Canal Co. to endow it. Congress never acted upon his wishes, however, and it wasn't until 1822 that the university that would eventually be named after the first president began to take shape. The private Columbian College in the District of Columbia opened that year with the aim of training students for the Baptist ministry. In 1904 the university shed its Baptist connections and changed its name to George Washington University. In 1912 it moved to its present location and since that time has become the second largest landholder in the District (after the federal government). Students have ranged from J. Edgar Hoover to Jacqueline Bouvier. In addition to modern university buildings GWU occupies many 19th-century houses. ⊠ *The downtown campus covers much of Foggy Bottom south of*

Pennsylvania Avenue between 19th and 24th Sts. Metro: Foggy Bottom.

⑭ Watergate. Thanks to the events that took place on the night of June 17, 1972, the Watergate is possibly the world's most notorious apartment-office complex. As Nixon aides E. Howard Hunt Jr. and G. Gordon Liddy sat in the Howard Johnson Motor Lodge across the street, five of their men were caught trying to bug the Democratic National Committee, headquartered on the sixth floor of the building, in an attempt to subvert the democratic process on behalf of the then president of the United States. (A marketing company occupies the space today.) ✉ *2600 Virginia Ave. Metro: Foggy Bottom.*

Alexandria

Just a short Metro ride (or bike ride) from Washington, Old Town Alexandria attracts visitors seeking a break from the monuments and hustle-and-bustle of the District. Founded in 1749 by Scottish merchants eager to capitalize on the booming tobacco trade, Alexandria emerged as one of the most important ports in Colonial America. The city's history is linked to the most significant events and personages of the Colonial and Revolutionary periods. This colorful past is still alive in restored 18th- and 19th-century homes, churches, and taverns; on the cobbled streets; and on the revitalized waterfront, where clipper ships dock and artisans display their wares.

The quickest way to get to Old Town is to take the Metro to the King Street stop (about 25 minutes from Metro Center). If you're driving you can take either the George Washington Memorial Parkway or Jefferson Davis Highway (Route 1) south from Arlington.

Numbers in the margin correspond to points of interest on the Old Town Alexandria, Virginia map.

Sights to See

⑪ Alexandria Black History Resource Center. The history of African Americans in Alexandria and Virginia from 1749 to the present is recounted here. Alexandria's history is hardly limited to the families of George Washington and Robert

E. Lee. The federal census of 1790 recorded 52 free blacks living in the city, and the port town was one of the largest slave exportation points in the South, with at least two bustling slave markets. ⊠ *638 N. Alfred St., ☎ 703/838–4356.* 🎟 *Free.* ⊙ *Tues.–Sat. 10–4.*

4 **Athenaeum.** One of the most noteworthy structures in Alexandria, the Athenaeum is a striking, reddish-brown Greek Revival edifice at the corner of Prince and Lee streets. It was built as a bank in the 1850s. ⊠ *201 Prince St.*

10 **Boyhood home of Robert E. Lee.** The childhood home in Alexandria of the commander in chief of the Confederate forces during the Civil War is a fine example of a 19th-century town house with Federal architecture and antique furnishings and paintings. ⊠ *607 Oronoco St., ☎ 703/548–8454.* 🎟 *$3.* ⊙ *Mon.–Sat. 10–4, Sun. 1–4; closed Dec. 15–Feb. 1 except on Sun. closest to Jan. 19 for Lee's birthday celebration; occasionally closed weekends for private events.*

5 **Captain's Row.** Many of Alexandria's sea captains once lived on this block. The cobblestones in the street were allegedly laid by Hessian mercenaries who had fought for the British during the Revolution and were held in Alexandria as prisoners of war. ⊠ *Prince St. between Lee and Union Sts.*

7 **Carlyle House.** The grandest of Alexandria's older houses, Carlyle House was patterned after a Scottish country manor house. The structure was completed in 1753 by Scottish merchant John Carlyle. This was General Braddock's headquarters and the place where he met with five royal governors in 1755 to plan the strategy and funding of the early campaigns of the French and Indian War. ⊠ *121 N. Fairfax St., ☎ 703/549–2997.* 🎟 *$3.* ⊙ *Tues.–Sat. 10–4:30, Sun. noon–4:40; tour every ½ hr.*

13 **Christ Church.** Both Washington and Lee were pewholders in this Alexandria, Virginia, church. (Washington paid 36 pounds and 10 shillings—a lot of money in those days—for Pew 60.) Built in 1773, Christ Church is a fine example of an English Georgian country-style church. It has a fine Palladian window, an interior balcony, and a wrought-brass-and-crystal chandelier brought from England at Wash-

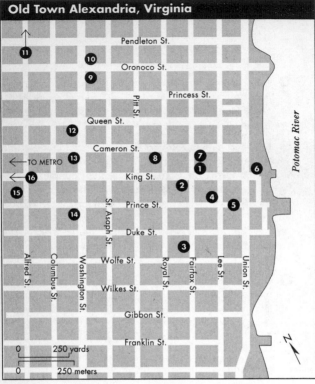

Old Town Alexandria, Virginia

Pendleton St.

Oronoco St.

Princess St.

Queen St.

Cameron St.

King St.

Prince St.

Duke St.

Wolfe St.

Wilkes St.

Gibbon St.

Franklin St.

Pitt St.

St. Asaph St.

Alfred St.

Columbus St.

Washington St.

Royal St.

Fairfax St.

Lee St.

Union St.

Potomac River

← TO METRO

0   250 yards
0   250 meters

Alexandria Black History Resource Center, **11**

Athenaeum, **4**

Boyhood home of Robert E. Lee, **10**

Captain's Row, **5**

Carlyle House, **7**

Christ Church, **13**

Friendship Fire House, **15**

Gadsby's Tavern Museum, **8**

George Washington Masonic National Memorial, **16**

Lee-Fendall House, **9**

Lloyd House, **12**

Lyceum, **14**

Old Presbyterian Meeting House, **3**

Ramsay House, **1**

Stabler-Leadbeater Apothecary, **2**

Torpedo Factory Arts Center, **6**

ington's expense. ⊠ *118 N. Washington St.,* ☎ *703/549–1450.* ⊞ *Free.* ⊙ *Weekdays 9–4, Sat. 9–4, Sun. 2–4:30; occasionally closed weekends for private events.*

Confederate Statue. In 1861, when Alexandria was occupied by Union forces, the 800 soldiers of the city's garrison marched out of town to join the Confederate Army. In the middle of Washington and Prince streets stands the Confederate Statue marking the point at which they assembled. In 1885 Confederate veterans proposed a memorial to honor their fallen comrades. This statue, based on John A. Elder's painting *Appomattox,* is of a lone soldier glumly surveying the battlefields after General Robert E. Lee's surrender. The names of 100 Alexandria Confederate dead are carved on the base.

⑮ **Friendship Fire House.** Alexandria's showcase firehouse is outfitted like a typical 19th-century firehouse. ⊠ *107 S. Alfred St.,* ☎ *703/838–3891.* ⊞ *Free.* ⊙ *Fri. and Sat. 10–4, Sun. 1–4.*

⑧ **Gadsby's Tavern Museum.** Gadsby's Tavern Museum is housed in the old City Tavern and Hotel, which was a center of political and social life in the late 18th century. George Washington attended birthday celebrations in the ballroom here. A tour of the facilities takes you through the taproom, dining room, assembly room, ballroom, and communal bedrooms. ⊠ *134 N. Royal St.,* ☎ *703/838–4242.* ⊞ *$3.* ⊙ *Oct.–Mar., Tues.–Sat. 11–4, Sun. 1–4 (last tour 3:15); Apr.–Sept., Tues.–Sat. 10–5, Sun. 1–5 (last tour 4:15); tours 15 mins before and 15 mins after the hr.*

⑯ **George Washington Masonic National Memorial.** Since Alexandria, like Washington, has no really tall buildings, the spire of the George Washington Masonic National Memorial dominates the surroundings and is visible for miles. The building fronts King Street, one of Alexandria's major east-west arteries; from the 9th-floor observation deck visitors get a spectacular view of Alexandria, with Washington in the distance. The building contains furnishings from the first Masonic lodge in Alexandria, in which George Washington was a member; he became a Mason in 1852 and was a Worshipful Master, a high rank, at the same time he served as president. ⊠ *101 Callahan Dr.,* ☎ *703/683–*

2007. ⌨ *Free.* ☉ *Daily 9–5; 50-min guided tour of building and observation deck daily at 9:30, 10:30, 11:30, 1, 2, 3, and 4.*

❾ Lee-Fendall House. The corner of Alexandria's Washington and Oronoco streets is known as Lee Corner because at one time a Lee-owned house stood on each of the four corners. Two survive. One is the Lee-Fendall House, the home of several illustrious members of the Lee family, including Richard Henry Lee, signer of the Declaration of Independence, and cavalry commander Henry "Light Horse Harry" Lee. ⊠ *614 Oronoco St.,* ☎ *703/548–1789.* ⌨ *$3.* ☉ *Tues.–Sat. 10–4, Sun. noon–4; occasionally closed weekends for private events.*

⓬ Lloyd House. A fine example of Georgian architecture, Lloyd House, built in 1797, is now operated as part of the Alexandria Library and houses a collection of rare books and documents relating to city and state history. ⊠ *220 N. Washington St.,* ☎ *703/838–4577.* ⌨ *Free.* ☉ *Mon.–Sat. 9–5.*

⓮ Lyceum. Built in 1839, the Lyceum served alternately as the Alexandria Library, a Civil War hospital, a residence, and an office building. It was restored in the 1970s and now houses three art galleries, a gift shop, and a museum devoted to the area's history. A limited amount of travel information for the entire state is also available here. ⊠ *201 S. Washington St.,* ☎ *703/838–4994.* ⌨ *Free.* ☉ *Mon.– Sat. 10–5, Sun. 1–5.*

❸ Old Presbyterian Meetinghouse. Built in 1774, the Old Presbyterian Meetinghouse was, as its name suggests, more than a church. It was a gathering place in Alexandria vital to Scottish patriots during the Revolution. Eulogies for George Washington were delivered here on December 29, 1799. In a corner of the churchyard you'll find the **Tomb of the Unknown Soldier of the American Revolution.** ⊠ *321 S. Fairfax St.,* ☎ *703/549–6670.* ⌨ *Free.* ☉ *Sanctuary weekdays 9–5 (if locked, obtain key from church office at 316 S. Royal St.).*

❶ Ramsay House. The best place to start a tour of Alexandria's Old Town is at the **Alexandria Convention & Visitors Bureau,** in Ramsay House, the home of the town's first

postmaster and lord mayor, William Ramsay. The structure
is believed to be the oldest house in Alexandria. Ramsay
was a Scotsman, as a swatch of his tartan on the door pro-
claims. Travel counselors here provide information,
brochures, and maps for self-guided walking tours. Visitors are given a 24-hour permit that allows them to park
free at any two-hour metered spot. ⊠ *221 King St., 22314,*
☎ *703/838–4200, TTY 703/838–6494.* ⊙ *Daily 9–5.*

❷ **Stabler-Leadbeater Apothecary.** Once patronized by George
Washington and the Lee family, Alexandria's Stabler-
Leadbeater Apothecary is the second-oldest apothecary in
the country. It was here, on October 17, 1859, that Lt. Col.
Robert E. Lee received orders to move to Harper's Ferry
to suppress John Brown's insurrection. The shop now
houses a small museum of 18th- and 19th-century apothecary memorabilia, including one of the finest collections of
apothecary bottles in the country (some 800 bottles in all).
⊠ *105–107 S. Fairfax St.,* ☎ *703/836–3713.* ☞ *$2.* ⊙
Mon.–Sat. 10–4, Sun. 1–5.

❻ **Torpedo Factory Arts Center.** A former munitions plant
(naval torpedoes were actually manufactured here during
World War I and World War II), now converted into stu-
dios and galleries for some 175 professional artists and artisans, the Torpedo Factory Arts Center is one of Alexandria's
most popular attractions. Almost every imaginable medium
is represented, from printmaking and sculpture to jewelry
making, pottery, and stained glass. Visitors can view the
workshops, and most of the art and crafts are for sale at
reasonable prices. ⊠ *105 N. Union St.,* ☎ *703/838–4565.*
☞ *Free.* ⊙ *Daily 10–5.*

Around Washington

The city and environs of Washington (including parts of
Maryland and Virginia) are dotted with worthwhile attractions that are outside the range of the walks presented
in this chapter. You may find some intriguing enough to go
a little out of your way to visit. The nearest Metro stop is
noted only if it's within reasonable walking distance of a
given sight.

Anacostia Museum. The richness of African-American culture is on display in the Anacostia museum, a Smithsonian museum in Southeast Washington's historic Anacostia neighborhood. Past exhibits have covered black inventors and aviators, the influential role of black churches, the history of the civil rights movement, African-American life in the antebellum South, and the beauty of African-American quilts. ⊠ *1901 Fort Pl. SE,* ☎ *202/287–3369.* ☞ *Free.* ⊙ *Daily 10–5. Metro: Navy Yard.*

Arlington National Cemetery. Some 250,000 American war dead, as well as many notable Americans (among them Presidents William Howard Taft and John F. Kennedy, General John Pershing, and Admiral Robert E. Peary) are interred in these 612 acres across the Potomac River from Washington, established as the nation's cemetery in 1864. While you are at Arlington you will probably hear the clear, doleful sound of a trumpet playing taps or the sharp reports of a gun salute. Approximately 15 funerals are held here daily. It is projected the cemetery will be filled in 2020.

To get there, you can take the Metro, travel on a Tourmobile bus, or walk across Memorial Bridge from the District (southwest of the Lincoln Memorial). If you're driving, there's a large paid parking lot at the skylit visitor center on Memorial Drive. Stop at the center for a free brochure with a detailed map of the cemetery. Tourmobile tour buses leave from just outside the visitor center April 1–September 30, daily 8:30–6:30; October 1–March 31, daily 8:30–4:30. You can buy tickets ($4) here for the 40-minute tour of the cemetery, which includes stops at the Kennedy grave sites, the Tomb of the Unknowns, and Arlington House. Touring the cemetery on foot means a fair bit of hiking. If you decide to walk, head west from the visitor center on Roosevelt Drive and then turn right on Weeks Drive. ⊠ *West end of Memorial Bridge, Arlington, VA,* ☎ *703/607–8052; to locate a specific grave* ☎ *703/697–2131.* ☞ *Free.* ⊙ *Apr.–Sept., daily 8–7; Oct.–Mar., daily 8–5.*

Franciscan Monastery and Gardens. Not far from the National Shrine of the Immaculate Conception (☞ *below*), the Byzantine-style Franciscan Monastery contains facsimiles of such Holy Land shrines as the Grotto of Bethlehem and the Holy Sepulcher. Underground are reproductions of the catacombs of Rome. The gardens are especially beautiful, planted with roses that bloom in summer. Take the Metro here from Union Station. ⊠ *14th and Quincy Sts. NE,* ☏ *202/526–6800.* ⊠ *Free.* ⊘ *Daily 9–5; catacombs tour on the hr (except noon) Mon.–Sat. 9–4, Sun. 1–4. Metro: Brookland–Catholic University.*

Frederick Douglass National Historic Site. Cedar Hill, the Anacostia home of abolitionist Frederick Douglass, was the first place designated by Congress as a Black National Historic Site. Douglass, an ex-slave who delivered fiery abolitionist speeches at home and abroad, resided here from 1877 until his death in 1895. The house has a wonderful view of the Federal City across the Anacostia River and contains many of Douglass's personal belongings. A short film on his life is shown at a nearby visitor center. ⊠ *1411 W St. SE,* ☏ *202/426–5961.* ⊠ *$3.* ⊘ *Mid-Oct.–mid-Apr., daily 9–4 (last tour at 3); mid-Apr.–mid-Oct., daily 9–5 (last tour at 4); tour on the hr. (except noon). Metro: Anacostia, then bus B2.*

Hillwood Museum. Hillwood House, cereal heiress Marjorie Merriweather Post's 40-room Georgian mansion in Washington, contains a large collection of 18th- and 19th-century French and Russian decorative art that includes gold and silver work, icons, lace, tapestries, china, and Fabergé eggs. Also on the estate are a dacha filled with Russian objects and an Adirondacks-style cabin that houses an assortment of Native American artifacts. The grounds are composed of lawns, formal French and Japanese gardens, and paths that wind through plantings of azaleas, laurels, and rhododendrons. Make reservations for the house tour well in advance. Hillwood is one or two Metro stops from the zoo, depending on which station you use. ⊠ *4155 Linnean Ave. NW,* ☏ *202/686–5807.* ⊠ *House and grounds $10; grounds only $2.* ⊘ *House tour Mar.–Jan., Tues.–Sat. 9:30–3; grounds Mar.–Jan., Tues.–Sat. 9–5. Metro: Van Ness/UDC.*

National Shrine of the Immaculate Conception. The largest Catholic church in the United States, the National Shrine of the Immaculate Conception was begun in 1920 and built with funds contributed by every parish in the country. Dedicated in 1959, the shrine is a blend of Romanesque and Byzantine styles, with a bell tower that reminds many of St. Mark's in Venice. Take the Metro here from Union Station. ✉ *Michigan Ave. and 4th St. NE,* ☎ *202/526-8300.* ☉ *Apr.–Oct., daily 7–7; Nov.–Mar., daily 7–6; Sat. vigil mass at 5:15; Sun. mass at 7:30, 9, 10:30, noon, 1:30 (in Latin), and 4:30. Metro: Brookland–Catholic University.*

National Zoological Park. Part of the Smithsonian Institution, the National Zoo is one of the foremost zoos in the world. Created by an Act of Congress in 1889, the 163-acre zoological park was designed by landscape architect Frederick Law Olmsted, the man who designed the U.S. Capitol grounds. For years the zoo's most famous residents were giant pandas Hsing-Hsing and Ling-Ling, gifts from China in 1972. But female Ling-Ling died of heart failure in 1993 at age 23. Though the zoo tried to fertilize some of Ling-Ling's extracted eggs, Hsing-Hsing is now the only giant panda in the United States.

The zoo has had breeding success with numerous other species, however, including red pandas, Pere David's deer, golden lion tamarins, and pygmy hippopotamuses. The only Komodo dragons in the country are at the National Zoo. Innovative compounds show many animals in naturalistic settings, including the Great Flight Cage—a walk-in aviary in which birds fly unrestricted. Zoolab, the Reptile Discovery Center, and the Bird Resource Center all offer activities that teach young visitors about biology. The most ambitious addition to the zoo is Amazonia, a reproduction of a South American rain forest ecosystem. The Cheetah Conservation Area is a grassy compound that's home to a family of the world's fastest cats. ✉ *3000 block of Connecticut Ave. NW,* ☎ *202/673–4800 or 202/673–4717.* 🎟 *Free.* ☉ *Apr. 15–Oct. 15, grounds daily 8–8, animal buildings daily 9–6, Amazonia daily 10–4; Oct. 16–Apr. 14, grounds daily 8–6, animal buildings daily 9–4:30, Amazonia daily 10–4:30. Metro: Cleveland Park or Woodley Park/Zoo.*

Newseum. The first and only museum dedicated to the news business opened in Arlington in April 1997. Here you can

In case you want to see the world.

At American Express, we're here to make your journey a smooth one. So we have over 1,700 travel service locations in over 120 countries ready to help. What else would you expect from the world's largest travel agency?

do more ®

AMERICAN
EXPRESS

Travel

http://www.americanexpress.com/travel

In case you want to be welcomed there.

We're here to see that you're always welcomed at establishments everywhere. That's why millions of people carry the American Express® Card – for peace of mind, confidence, and security, around the world or just around the corner.

do more

AMERICAN EXPRESS

Cards

In case you're running low.

We're here to help with more than 118,000 Express Cash locations around the world. In order to enroll, just call American Express before you start your vacation.

do more

AMERICAN EXPRESS

Express Cash

And just in case.

We're here with American Express® Travelers Cheques
and Cheques *for Two*® They're the safest way to carry
money on your vacation and the surest way to get a
refund, practically anywhere, anytime.
Another way we help you...

do more®

AMERICAN
EXPRESS

**Travelers
Cheques**

relive recent history's defining moments; learn how the business of journalism evolved; try your hand at reporting, anchoring, and weathercasting; see artifacts like Ernie Pyle's typewriter and Columbus's letter to Queen Isabella about discovering the New World; and catch the latest breaking news from around the world. The Newseum can be reached by foot from the Key Bridge; it is two blocks from the Rosslyn metro. ✉ *1101 Wilson Blvd.,* ☎ *888/639–7386.* ⛄ *Free.* ☉ *Wed.–Sun. 10–5. Metro: Rosslyn.*

Pentagon. Composed of not one but five concentric buildings, collectively as wide as three Washington Monuments laid end to end, the Pentagon is the largest office building in the world. The buildings are connected by 17½ mi of corridors through which 23,000 military and civilian personnel pass each day. There are 691 drinking fountains, 7,754 windows, and a blizzard of other eye-popping statistics. Astonishingly, all this was completed in 1943 after just two years of construction.

The escalator from the Pentagon Metro station surfaces right into the gargantuan office building. The 75-minute tour of the Pentagon takes you past only those areas that are meant to be seen by outside visitors. In other words, you won't see situation rooms, communications centers, or gigantic maps outlining U.S. and foreign troop strengths. A uniformed serviceman or -woman (who conducts the entire tour walking backward, lest anyone slip away down a corridor) will take you past hallways lined with the portraits of past and present military leaders, scale models of Air Force planes and Navy ships, and the Hall of Heroes, where the names of all the Congressional Medal of Honor winners are inscribed. Occasionally you will catch a glimpse through an interior window of the Pentagon's 5-acre interior courtyard. A photo ID is required for admission; children under 16 must be accompanied by an adult. ✉ *Off I–395, Arlington, VA,* ☎ *703/695–1776.* ⛄ *Free.* ☉ *Tour weekdays every ½ hr 9:30–3:30.*

Washington Doll's House and Toy Museum. A collection of American and imported dolls, dollhouses, toys, and games, most from the Victorian period, fills a compact museum founded in 1975 by a dollhouse historian. Miniature accessories, dollhouse kits, and antique toys and games are on sale in the museum's shops. Dumbarton Oaks is the nearest Georgetown sight. ⊠ *5236 44th St. NW,* ☎ *202/244–0024.* ⊠ *$4.* ⊙ *Tues.–Sat. 10–5, Sun. noon–5. Metro: Friendship Heights.*

Washington National Cathedral. Construction of Washington National Cathedral, a stunning Gothic church—the sixth-largest cathedral in the world—started in 1907 and was finished on September 30, 1990, when the building was consecrated. Like its 14th-century counterparts, the National Cathedral (officially **Washington's Cathedral Church of St. Peter and St. Paul**) has a nave, flying buttresses, transepts, and vaults that were built stone by stone. It is adorned with fanciful gargoyles created by skilled stone carvers. The tomb of Woodrow Wilson, the only president buried in Washington, is on the south side of the nave. The expansive view of the city from the Pilgrim Gallery is exceptional. ⊠ *Wisconsin and Massachusetts Aves. NW,* ☎ *202/537–6200, 202/537–6207 tour information.* ⊠ *Suggested donation for tour $2.* ⊙ *Fall, winter, and spring, daily 10–4:30; Memorial Day–Labor Day, weekdays 10–9, weekends 10–4:30; Sun. services at 8, 9, 10, 11, and 6:30; evensong at 4; tours Mon.–Sat. 10–3:15, Sun. 12:30–2:45.*

3 Dining

By
Deborah
Papier

Updated
by Holly
Bass

AS THE NATION'S CAPITAL, Washington finds itself playing host to an international array of visitors and new residents. This constant infusion of new cultures means that District restaurants are getting better and better. Despite the dearth of ethnic neighborhoods and the kinds of restaurant districts found in many cities, you *can* find almost any type of food here, from Nepalese to Salvadoran to Ethiopian. Even the French-trained chefs who have traditionally set the standard in fine dining are turning to health-conscious New American cuisine, spicy Southwestern recipes, or appetizer-size Spanish dishes called *tapas* for new inspiration.

In the city's one officially recognized ethnic enclave, Chinatown (centered on G and H streets NW between 6th and 8th; Metro: Gallery Place), Burmese, Thai, and other Asian cuisines add variety to the many traditional Chinese restaurants. Aside from Chinatown, the following areas of the city have concentrations of restaurants:

Most of the deluxe restaurants are **downtown** near K Street NW, also the location of many of the city's blue-chip law firms. These are the restaurants that feed off expense-account diners and provide the most elegant atmosphere, most attentive service, and often the best food. In the **old downtown district,** visitors with children can take advantage of the many sandwich shops geared to office workers to grab a quick bite during the day, but will find far fewer choices evenings and weekends. However, the entire downtown area is in a state of flux gastronomically, with famed restaurants like Jean-Louis in the Watergate closing their doors and new ones blossoming. Trendy microbrewery/restaurants and cigar lounges are part of the new wave.

Another popular restaurant district is **Georgetown,** whose central intersection is Wisconsin Avenue and M Street. Here you'll find white-tablecloth establishments next door to hole-in-the-wall joints. Restaurants in the adjacent **West End** are worth checking out as well. This area, bounded roughly by Rock Creek Park to the west, N Street to the north, 20th Street to the east, and K Street to the south, is increasingly bridging the gap between Georgetown and downtown restaurant zones. Heading north from Georgetown on Wisconsin Avenue, you'll find a cluster of good restaurants in the **Glover Park** area, including the city's best sushi bar, Sushi-Ko.

An exuberantly diverse culinary competitor to Georgetown is **Adams-Morgan.** Eighteenth Street NW extending south from Columbia Road is wall-to-wall restaurants, with new ones opening so fast it's almost impossible to track them. Although the area has retained some of its Hispanic identity, the new eating establishments tend to be Asian, New American (traditional American ingredients given a French turn), Italian, and Ethiopian. Parking can be impossible on weekends. **Woodley Park** has culinary temptations of its own, with a lineup of popular ethnic restaurants.

Some of the city's best upscale Italian restaurants are in **Dupont Circle.** You'll also find a variety of cafés, most with outdoor seating. The District's better gay-friendly establishments are here as well, especially along 17th Street. Chains like Starbucks and Hannibal's have put fancy coffee on every corner, but long-established espresso bars, like the 24-hour Afterwords (located within a bookstore), are a better source for breakfast and light or late fare.

Capitol Hill has a number of bar-eateries that cater to Congressional types in need of fortification after a day spent running the country. The dining possibilities on Capitol Hill are boosted by Union Station, which contains some decent—if pricey—restaurants like B. Smith's and America.

The restaurants in many of the city's luxury hotels are another source of fine dining. The Willard Inter-Continental hotel's formal dining room, the former Ritz-Carlton's Jockey Club, and the Morrison-Clark Inn's dining room are especially noteworthy. The cuisine is often artful and fresh, with special care given to ingredients, preparation, and presentation. Of course, such attention to detail comes at a price.

CATEGORY	COST*
$$$$	over $35
$$$	$26–$35
$$	$15–$25
$	under $15

per person for a three-course meal, excluding drinks, service, and sales tax (10% in D.C., 4.5%–9% in VA, 5% in MD)

Adams-Morgan/Woodley Park

African

$$ ✕ **Bukom Café.** Sunny African pop music, a palm-frond-and-*kente*-cloth decor, and a spicy West African menu brighten this narrow two-story dining room. Appetizers include *moi-moi* (black-eyed peas, tomatoes, and corned beef) and *nklakla* (tomato soup with goat). Entrées range from *egussi* (goat with melon seeds) to *kumasi* (chicken in a peanut sauce) to vegetarian dishes such as *jollof* rice and fried plantains. Live music nightly and late hours (until 2 AM Wednesday, Thursday, and Sunday; until 3 AM Friday–Saturday) keep this place hopping. ⊠ *2442 18th St. NW,* ☎ *202/265–4600. AE, D, MC, V. Closed Mon. No lunch.*

Brazilian

$$–$$$ ✕ **Grill from Ipanema.** The Grill focuses on Brazilian cuisine, from spicy seafood stews to grilled steak and other hearty meat dishes. Appetizers include fried yuca with spicy sausages and—for adventurous eaters—fried alligator. Second Lady Tipper Gore adores the *mexilhao a carioca,* garlicky mussels cooked in a clay pot. Traditional feijoada—a stew of black beans, pork, and smoked meat—is served Wednesday, Saturday, and Sunday. ⊠ *1858 Columbia Rd. NW,* ☎ *202/986–0757. AE, D, DC, MC, V. No lunch weekdays.*

Chinese

$$ ✕ **City Lights of China.** The Art Deco City Lights of China
★ makes the top restaurant critics' lists every year. The traditional Chinese fare is excellent. Less common specialties are deftly cooked, as well, among them lamb in a tangy peppery sauce and shark's fin soup. Delicious jumbo shrimp are baked in their shells before being quickly stir-fried with ginger and spices. The mint-green booths and elegant silk

flower arrangements conjure up breezy spring days, even in the midst of a frenzied dinner rush. ⊠ *1731 Connecticut Ave., NW,* ☎ *202/265–6688. AE, D, DC, MC, V.*

Ethiopian

$–$$ ✕ **Meskerem.** Ethiopian cuisine abounds in Adams-
★ Morgan, but Meskerem is distinctive for its bright dining room and the balcony where you can eat Ethiopian-style—seated on the floor on leather cushions, with large woven baskets for tables. Entrées are served on a large piece of *injera,* a sourdough flatbread; diners eat family style by scooping up mouthful-size portions of the hearty dishes with extra bread. Among Meskerem's specialties are delicious stews made with spicy *berbere* chili sauce; *kitfo,* a buttery beef dish served raw like steak tartare or very rare; and a tangy, green chili vinaigrette potato salad. ⊠ *2434 18th St. NW,* ☎ *202/462–4100. AE, DC, MC, V.*

Italian

$$ ✕ **Pasta Mia.** Pasta Mia's southern Italian appetizers and entrées all cost a palatable $7–$9. Large bowls of steaming pasta are served with a generous layer of fresh-grated Parmesan. Best-sellers include fusilli with broccoli and whole cloves of roasted garlic, rich fettuccine verde, and spicy penne *arrabiata* (marinara sauce with olives). Tiramisu, served in a teacup with espresso-soaked ladyfingers, is an elegant way to finish a meal. ⊠ *1790 Columbia Rd. NW,* ☎ *202/328–9114. MC, V. Closed Sun. No lunch.*

Latin American/Spanish

$$–$$$ ✕ **Lauriol Plaza.** A charming corner enclave on the border of Adams-Morgan and Dupont Circle, Lauriol Plaza serves Latin American and Spanish dishes—seviche, paella, and so on—in winning combinations. Such rustic entrées as Cuban-style pork and *lomo saltado* (Peruvian-style strip steak with onions, tomatoes, and fiery jalapeño peppers) are specialties. The simply decorated dining room, with white tablecloths and white walls enlivened by gilt-framed paintings, can get noisy; the alfresco terrace is preferable in good weather. ⊠ *1801 18th St. NW,* ☎ *202/387–0035. AE, D, DC, MC, V.*

Washington Dining

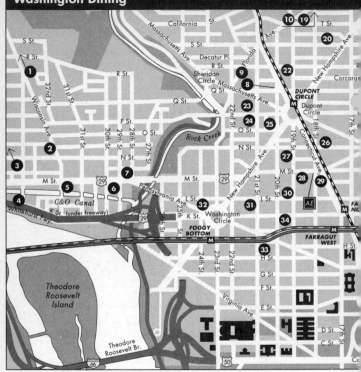

B. Smith's, **46**

Bistro
Français, **5**

Bombay
Club, **35**

Bukom
Café, **13**

Burma, **47**

Café Asia, **30**

Café
Japone, **24**

Citronelle, **6**

City Lights of
China, **22**

Coco Loco, **49**

Gabriel, **23**

Galileo, **31**

Georgia
Brown's, **36**

Gerard's
Place, **37**

Grill from
Ipanema, **15**

Heart &
Soul, **44**

Hibiscus
Café, **4**

i Ricchi, **27**

Jaleo, **42**

Kinkhead's, **33**

La
Chaumière, **7**

La Colline, **43**

Lauriol
Plaza, **20**

Le Lion
D'Or, **29**

Lebanese
Taverna, **10**

Li Ho, **48**

Mama
Ayesha's
Restaurant, **12**

Malaysian

$$–$$$ ✕ **Straits of Malaya.** Just far enough away from Dupont Circle to be quaint, Straits of Malaya serves some of the most exotic food in Washington—Malaysian/Singaporean cuisine that borrows from Chinese, Thai, and Indian cooking. Dishes—among them chicken *satay* (on skewers), five-spice rolls, fiery *laksa* (noodle soup), *udang goreng* (shrimp in a coconut milk sauce), and *poh pia* (shredded jicama stir-fried with vegetables)—are lovely combinations of sweet and pepper-hot spices. ⊠ *1836 18th St. NW,* ☎ *202/483–1483. AE, MC, V. No lunch weekends.*

Mediterranean

$$–$$$ ✕ **TomTom.** TomTom's trendy menu features pizza baked in a wood-burning oven and tapas of all sorts. Lighter fare such as green salads topped with shrimp or grilled chicken is also available. And desserts range from the sinful *boca negra,* a baked chocolate truffle topped with cinnamon whipped cream, to light sorbets served in the skins of fruit. But the real draw is the atmosphere. On warm nights the rooftop is packed and area artists set up easels to paint while patrons watch. Hip, artsy crowds wait almost an hour on weekends for tables. ⊠ *2333 18th St. NW,* ☎ *202/588–1300. AE, D, DC, MC, V. No lunch.*

Mexican

$–$$ ✕ **Mixtec.** Don't expect tortilla chips as a starter—they simply don't serve them. They do, however, offer a trio of delicious salsas to season their array of authentic dishes. *Tacos al carbon* are simple and perfect. Unlike their fast food counterparts that are topped with lettuce and cheese, these consist only of grilled beef or pork and fresh corn tortillas; grilled spring onions are a nice accompaniment. Fajitas, enchiladas, and seafood are cooked in the regional styles of Veracruz, Mazatlán, and Acapulco, which the menu does a good job of explaining. The *licuados* (homemade fruit shakes) are refreshing complements to the sometimes spicy dishes. ⊠ *1792 Columbia Rd. NW,* ☎ *202/332–1011. No reservations. MC, V.*

Middle Eastern

$$–$$$ ✕ **Lebanese Taverna.** High, arched ceilings, cedar panels etched with intricate leaf patterns, and woven rugs give the Taverna a feeling of warm elegance. Be sure to start your

meal with an order of Arabic bread that's baked in a wood-burning oven. Small, fried pies filled with spinach, cheese, or meat are buttery and surprisingly light. Lamb, beef, chicken, and seafood is either grilled on kabobs, slow-roasted and carved for *shawarma,* or smothered with a garlicky yogurt sauce. Pomegranate seeds are sprinkled on top of many dishes for a colorful accent. A glass of Arak, a strong, anise-flavored liquor makes an excellent digestif. ✉ *2641 Connecticut Ave. NW,* ☎ *202/265–8681;* ✉ *5900 Washington Blvd., Arlington, VA,* ☎ *703/241–8681. AE, D, DC, MC, V.*

$–$$ ✗ **Mama Ayesha's Restaurant.** Journalists and politicians (autographed pictures of the last two presidents hang prominently) are known to frequent Ayesha's for the reasonably priced fare. At the family-run eatery, staples like chicken and lamb kabobs can be had for less than $10, baskets of complimentary pita bread are served hot, and the crisp falafels are some of the best in town. Weekends bring Arabic bands and belly dancing. ✉ *1967 Calvert St. NW,* ☎ *202/232–5431. AE, DC, MC, V.*

New American

$$$ ✗ **Nora.** Although it bills itself as an "organic restaurant," Nora is no collective-run juice bar. The food is sophisticated and attractive, like the quilt-decorated dining room. Peppered beef carpaccio with manchego cheese is a good starter. Entrées—seared rockfish with artichoke broth; grilled lamb chops with white-bean ragout; and risotto topped with winter vegetables, to name some past favorites—exemplify the chef's emphasis on well-balanced, complex ingredients. Chocolate-orange cake with blood-orange segments and pear-and-blueberry crisp with praline ice cream are among the sublime desserts. ✉ *2132 Florida Ave. NW,* ☎ *202/462–5143. MC, V. Closed Sun. No lunch.*

Thai

$–$$$ ✗ **Thai Flavor.** Though you can get a satisfying meal at any of the Thai restaurants dotting the Woodley Park area, Thai Flavor offers the best value and atmosphere, with its wide front window, exposed brick walls, and pleasant staff. You'll find items like traditional *pad thai* noodles, tangy lemongrass soup, crisp tempura vegetables, and honey-sweetened garlic chicken at their constantly replenished buffet table ($7.95 for lunch, a dollar more for dinner). A few extra dollars gives you access to the sushi buffet upstairs. You can also order à la carte from the extensive menu. ⊠ *2605 Connecticut Ave., NW,* ☎ *202/745–2000. AE, D, DC, MC, V.*

Capitol Hill

American

$$–$$$$ ✕ **Monocle.** The fireplaces and political portraits in this restaurant in two town houses add to the aura of cozy tradition. Monocle is still probably the best place in Washington for spotting members of Congress at lunch and dinner. The cooking—regional American cuisine—is adequate if unexciting and a so-so value: The old-style Capitol Hill atmosphere is the real draw. Seafood is a specialty; try the crab cakes, and take advantage of the fresh fish specials. ⊠ *107 D St. NE,* ☎ *202/546–4488. AE, DC, MC, V. Closed weekends.*

French

$$$–$$$$ ✕ **La Colline.** Chef Robert Gréault has worked to make La
   ★   Colline one of the city's best French restaurants. The seasonal menu emphasizes market-fresh vegetables and seafood, with offerings ranging from simple grilled preparations to fricassees and gratins with imaginative sauces. Other offerings include duck with orange or cassis sauce and veal with chanterelle mushrooms. ⊠ *400 N. Capitol St. NW,* ☎ *202/ 737–0400. AE, DC, MC, V. Closed Sun. No lunch Sat.*

Seafood

$$–$$$ ✕ **Phillip's Flagship.** Cavernous rooms and capacious decks overlook the Capital Yacht Club's marina. There's a sushi bar (Monday–Saturday), a party room with its own deck, and space for 1,400. Despite its size, Phillips Flagship serves excellent seafood with dispatch. Succulent soft-shell crabs and blackened catfish are accompanied by chunky fresh vegetables cooked to crunchy perfection. ⊠ *900 Water St. SW,* ☎ *202/488–8515. AE, D, DC, MC, V.*

Southern

$$–$$$$ ✕ **B. Smith's.** For appetizers, try the grilled cheddar cheese grits, jambalaya, or crisp spring rolls with mango and wasabi dipping sauces—but skip the overly breaded fried green tomatoes and the too-sweet sweet potatoes. Signature entrée Swamp Thing may not be pretty, but this mix of mustard-seasoned shrimp and crawfish with collard greens is delicious. Seafood and anything with barbecue sauce is highly recommended. Desserts are comforting classics, slightly dressed up: pumpkin pound cake with praline sauce, warm bread pudding, and sweet potato pecan pie. ⊠ *50 Massachusetts Ave. NE, inside Union Station,* ☎ *202/ 289–6188. AE, D, DC, MC, V.*

$–$$ ✕ **Heart & Soul.** The extensive menu gives Southern favorites a Caribbean/Creole flair. You can order your catfish blackened or corn-fried and enjoy chicken wings cooked with Jamaican spices or with barbecue sauce. It's easy to make a meal out of the delicious sides: mashed potatoes, red beans and rice, candied sweet potatoes, collard greens, and black-eyed peas. The service, while friendly, can be very slow, so plan accordingly. ⊠ *424 8th St. SE,* ☎ *202/546–8801. AE, MC, V.*

Downtown

American

$$$–$$$$ ✕ **Sam and Harry's.** Cigar-friendly Sam and Harry's is understated, genteel, and packed at lunch and dinner. Although the miniature crab cakes are a good way to begin, the main attractions are their selection of prime meats like the porterhouse and New York strip steaks served on the bone. For those who've sworn off beef, daily seafood specials include Maine lobster. End the meal with warm pecan pie laced with melted chocolate. ⊠ *1200 19th St. NW,* ☎ *202/296– 4333. AE, D, DC, MC, V. Closed Sun. No lunch Sat.*

$$–$$$ ✕ **Old Ebbitt Grill.** People flock here to drink at the several bars, which seem to go on for miles, and to enjoy the oyster bar and carefully prepared bar food that includes buffalo chicken wings, hamburgers, and Reuben sandwiches. But this is not just a place for casual nibbling; the Old Ebbitt offers serious diners homemade pastas and daily specials until 1 AM, emphasizing fish dishes and steak. Despite the crowds, the restaurant never feels cramped, thanks to its well-spaced, comfortable booths. Service can be slow at lunch. Those in a hurry will prefer the quick, café-style Ebbitt

Express next door. ⊠ *675 15th St. NW,* ☎ *202/347–4800. AE, D, DC, MC, V.*

$ ✕ **Sholl's Colonial Cafeteria.** Their slogan is, "Where good foods are prepared right, served right, and priced right"— and truer words were never spoken. Suited federal workers line up next to pensioners and visiting students to grab a bite at this Washington institution, where favorites include chopped steak, liver and onions, and baked chicken and fish for less than $5. Sholl's is famous for its apple, blueberry, peach, and other fruit pies: All the desserts are scrumptious and cost around $1. ⊠ *1990 K St. NW,* ☎ *202/ 296–3065. No credit cards. No dinner Sun.*

Asian

$$ ✕ **Burma.** That Burma (now officially called Myanmar) the country is bordered by India, Thailand, and China gives some indication of the cuisine at Burma the restaurant, an exquisite jewel in fading Chinatown. Here curry and tamarind share pride of place with lemon, cilantro, and soy seasonings. Batter-fried eggplant and squash are deliciously paired with complex, peppery sauces. Green Tea Leaf and other salads leave the tongue with a pleasant tingle. Such entrées as mango pork, tamarind fish, and Kokang chicken are equally satisfying. ⊠ *740 6th St. NW, 2nd floor,* ☎ *202/ 638–1280. AE, D, DC, MC, V. No lunch weekends.*

$–$$ ✕ **Café Asia.** One of Washington's best pan-Asian restaurants, Café Asia presents Japanese, Chinese, Thai, Singaporean, Indonesian, Malaysian, and Vietnamese variations on succulent themes. Highlights include Indonesian sweet-and-sour shrimp, moist satays, spicy fish in banana leaves, and noodle soups. Weekday evenings, enjoy cheap drinks and eats during the sushi happy hour. The dining area covers three floors, the decor is spartan, and the staff is small, but low prices and the chance to try many different types of food make waits worthwhile. ⊠ *1134 19th St. NW,* ☎ *202/659–2696. AE, DC, MC, V. No lunch Sun.*

Chinese

$–$$ ✕ **Li Ho.** Head for unassuming Li Ho if good food in satisfying portions is what you seek. Some locals prefer neighboring Full Kee (⊠ *509 H St. NW,* ☎ *202/371–2233*), which has a competitive assortment of Cantonese-style roasted meats, but Li Ho's specialties—including duck soup with mustard greens and Singapore noodles, a rice noodle dish seasoned with curry and bits of meat—are favorites among the lunchtime crowd. ⊠ *501 H St. NW,* ☎ *202/289–2059. MC, V.*

French

$$$$
★ ✕ **Le Lion D'Or.** If you've ever wondered why so many gourmets rave about French food, Le Lion D'Or's lobster soufflé, crepes with oysters and caviar, ravioli with foie gras, salmon with crayfish, and roast pigeon with mushrooms provide delectable answers. The fabulous dessert soufflés may be filled with raspberries or orange essence; or try the sinful chocolate soufflé surrounded by vanilla crème anglaise. ⊠ *1150 Connecticut Ave. NW, entrance on 18th St. NW,* ☎ *202/296–7972. Jacket and tie. AE, DC, MC, V. Reservations essential. Closed Sun. No lunch.*

Indian

$$–$$$
★ ✕ **Bombay Club.** One block from the White House, the beautiful Bombay Club tries to re-create the kind of solace the Beltway elite might have found in a private club had they been 19th-century British colonials in India rather than late-20th-century Washingtonians. The bar, which serves hot hors d'oeuvres at cocktail hour, is furnished with rattan chairs and paneled with dark wood. The dining room, with potted palms and a bright blue ceiling above white plaster moldings, is elegant and decorous. Though the menu includes unusual seafood specialties and a large number of vegetarian dishes, the real standouts are the breads and the seafood appetizers. ⊠ *815 Connecticut Ave. NW,* ☎ *202/659–3727. AE, DC, MC, V. No lunch Sat.*

International

$$$–$$$$
★ ✕ **Gerard's Place.** With a main dining room strikingly colored in gray and burnt umber, Gerard's Place concentrates on such fresh, intriguingly prepared entrées as poached lobster with a ginger, lime, and Sauternes sauce; venison served with dried fruits and pumpkin and beetroot purees; and seared tuna with black olives and roasted red peppers. Desserts like the chocolate tear, a teardrop-shaped flourless chocolate cake veined with raspberry, are exquisite. ⊠ *915 15th St. NW,* ☎ *202/737–4445. AE, MC, V. Closed Sun. No lunch Sat.*

Italian

$$$–$$$$ ✕ **Galileo.** A spacious, popular restaurant with homemade
★ everything—from bread sticks to mozzarella—Galileo serves
risotto, a long list of grilled fish, a game bird dish (such as
quail, guinea hen, or woodcock), and at least one or two
beef or veal dishes. Preparations are generally simple. For
example, the veal chop might be served with mushroom-
and-rosemary sauce, the beef with black-olive sauce and po-
lenta. ⊠ *1110 21st St. NW,* ☎ *202/293–7191. AE, D, DC,
MC, V. No lunch weekends.*

$$$–$$$$ ✕ **i Ricchi.** An airy dining room decorated with terra-cotta
★ tiles, cream-colored archways, and floral frescoes, i Ric-
chi is priced for expense accounts and remains a favorite
of critics and upscale crowds for its earthy Tuscan cuisine.
The spring/summer menu includes such offerings as rolled
pork and rabbit roasted in wine and fresh herbs, and
skewered shrimp; the fall/winter bill of fare brings grilled
lamb chops, thick soups, and sautéed beef fillet. ⊠ *1220
19th St. NW,* ☎ *202/835–0459. AE, DC, MC, V. Closed
Sun. No lunch Sat.*

Moroccan

$$ ✕ **Marrakesh.** Come here for a bit of Morocco in a part of
★ the city better known for auto-supply shops. The menu is a
fixed-price ($22) feast shared by everyone at your table and
eaten without silverware (flatbread, served with the meal, is
used as a scoop). Appetizers consist of a platter of three sal-
ads followed by *b'stella,* a chicken version of Morocco's traditional pigeon pie. For the first main course, choose from
several chicken preparations. A beef or lamb dish is served
next, followed by vegetable couscous, fresh fruit, mint tea,
and pastries. Belly dancers put on a nightly show. ⊠ *617 New
York Ave. NW,* ☎ *202/393–9393. Reservations essential.
No credit cards. Lunch only for large groups by reservation.*

New American

$$$–$$$$ ✕ **Kinkead's.** Kinkead's multichambered dining room in-
cludes a downstairs pub and raw bar with American-style
tapas and other inexpensive fare. Upstairs, watch Kinkead
and company turn out grilled dishes (the squid is scrump-
tious) with garden salsas, New England–inspired appetiz-
ers and seafood soups, and savory meat and fowl dishes.
For a refreshing finish, the light cool tang of homemade sor-

bet is just the thing. ⊠ *2000 Pennsylvania Ave. NW,* ☎ *202/ 296–7700. AE, DC, MC, V.*

$$–$$$$ ✕ **Occidental Grill.** In the stately Willard hotel complex, the popular Occidental Grill offers innovative and artful dishes, attentive service, and photos of politicians past and present. Grilled options include poultry, steak, and fish; salmon, for instance, might be grilled and served with crab hash in a saffron-fennel broth. ⊠ *1475 Pennsylvania Ave. NW,* ☎ *202/783–1475. AE, DC, MC, V.*

South American

$$–$$$ ✕ **Coco Loco.** One of the hot spots in the "Pennsylvania Quarter" area, Coco Loco's big draw is Mexican tapas, appetizer-size snacks of endless variety that are generally washed down with wine or beer. Favorites include shrimp stuffed with white cheese and wrapped in bacon, duck enchiladas, and *chiles rellenos* (stuffed chilis) in a tomato-cream puree. If you're into serious meat-eating, try the Brazilian-style *churrasqueria*—a parade of skewered grilled meats that are brought to your table and sliced right onto your plate. Wednesday through Saturday night, half the restaurant becomes an upscale nightclub. ⊠ *810 7th St. NW,* ☎ *202/ 289–2626. AE, MC, V. Closed Sun. No lunch Sat.*

Southern

$$–$$$ ✕ **Georgia Brown's.** An elegant "New South" eatery, Georgia Brown's serves shrimp Carolina-style (with the head on and steaming grits on the side), beef tenderloin medallions with a bourbon-pecan sauce, thick rich crab soup, and specials like grilled salmon and smoked-bacon green beans. Fried green tomatoes are given the gourmet treatment, as is sweet potato cheesecake. ⊠ *950 15th St. NW,* ☎ *202/ 393–4499. AE, DC, MC, V. No lunch Sat.*

Southwestern/Tex-Mex

$$$–$$$$ ✕ **Red Sage.** Near the White House is an upscale rancher's delight, roping in the likes of George Bush and Bill Clinton for the tony chow. The multimillion-dollar decor has a barbed-wire-and-lizard theme and a pseudo-adobe warren of dining rooms. Upstairs is the chili bar and café, where thrifty trendsetters can enjoy the comparatively inexpensive sandwiches and appetizers. Downstairs, owner Mark Miller's Berkeley-Santa Fe background surfaces in elaborate, artful presentations such as roasted Virginia buf-

falo with wild shrimp or stuffed game birds topped with mushroom-jerky salsa. ⊠ *605 14th St. NW,* ☎ *202/638–4444. AE, D, DC, MC, V. No lunch Sun.*

Spanish

$$–$$$ ✕ **Jaleo.** A lively Spanish bistro, Jaleo encourages you to
★ make a meal out of its long list of hot and cold tapas, although such entrées as grilled fish and paella—which comes in three different versions—are just as tasty. Highlights of the tapas menu are *gambas al ajillo* (sautéed garlic shrimp), fried potatoes with spicy tomato sauce, and *pinchitos* (a skewer of grilled chorizo) with garlic mashed potatoes. For dessert, don't miss the crisp and buttery apple charlotte and the chocolate hazelnut tart. ⊠ *480 7th St. NW,* ☎ *202/628–7949. AE, D, MC, V.*

Dupont Circle

Italian

$$$–$$$$ ✕ **Vincenzo al Sole.** Here's something rather rare: a restaurant that has lowered its prices while continuing to offer many of the same dishes with no change in quality. The emphasis is on simply prepared seafood dishes such as *merluzzo alla calabrese* (roasted cod with capers and olives) and *branzino al salmoriglio* (grilled rockfish with oregano). The menu also includes meat and game dishes such as roast duck with polenta. Part of the dining room is in an airy, glass-roof courtyard. ⊠ *1606 20th St. NW,* ☎ *202/667–0047. AE, DC, MC, V. Closed Sun. No lunch Sat.*

Japanese

$$–$$$ ✕ **Café Japone.** Café Japone's dark interior has an alternative-scene edge. On most weeknights after 10 PM you're likely to find Japanese businessmen and students, happy from good food and bottles of hot sake, belting out the latest Asian pop songs while a karaoke sound system provides musical backup. Thursday nights, there's a live jazz band and a mellower crowd. The sushi is nothing to rave about, but it's good, and the kitchen stays open until 1:30 AM during the week, 2:30 AM on weekends. Steamed wontons and crispy fried *age dofu* (tofu in a soy broth) are tasty appetizers. Even nonvegetarians will enjoy the vegetable plate. ⊠ *2032 P St. NW,* ☎ *202/223–1573. AE, MC, V. No lunch.*

Middle Eastern

$ ✗ **Skewers/Café Luna.** As the name implies, the focus at Skewers is on kabobs, here served with almond-flaked rice or pasta. Lamb with eggplant and chicken with roasted pepper are the most popular variations, but vegetable kabobs and skewers of filet mignon and shrimp are equally tasty. With nearly 20 choices, the appetizer selection is huge. If the restaurant is too crowded, you can enjoy the cheap eats (shrimp and avocado salad, mozzarella and tomato sandwiches, vegetable lasagna, pizza, and salads) downstairs at Café Luna (☎ 202/387–4005) or the reading room–coffeehouse upstairs at Luna Books (☎ 202/332–2543). ⊠ *1633 P St. NW, ☎ 202/387–7400. AE, DC, MC, V.*

New American

$$$–$$$$ ✗ **Tabard Inn.** The Tabard Inn (☞ Chapter 4) meshes an old European look—fading portraits, doilies—with '60s values, serving only organic produce and meat to its baby boomer clientele. Appetizers have included smoked trout cakes with chili-basil mayonnaise, while saffron linguine in a tomato-pepper fumet with salmon, oysters, and monkfish is a good example of a colorful main course. Desserts like warm strawberry-rhubarb crisp and white-chocolate cheesecake get raves. The pretty courtyard is open in clement weather. ⊠ *1739 N St. NW, ☎ 202/833–2668. MC, V.*

South American/Spanish

$$$ ✗ **Gabriel.** Gabriel takes a nouvelle approach to traditional Latin American and Spanish dishes. *Pupusas,* Salvadoran meat patties, are filled with chorizo and grilled scallops. Grilled ancho shrimp comes with a sweet potato-green onion tamale. While you may prefer to order à la carte, the extensive tapas buffets, for lunch and happy hour, are sure winners. The brunch buffet is truly outstanding with its made-to-order quesadillas and Mediterranean specialties like seafood paella, cassoulet, and salads. The dessert table offers tiny fruit tarts, various cheesecakes, cookies, and decadent chocolate items. ⊠ *2121 P St. NW, ☎ 202/956–6690. AE, D, DC, MC, V.*

Thai

$–$$ ✗ **Sala Thai.** Who says Thai food has to be scalp-sweating hot? Sala Thai will make the food as spicy as you wish, but the chef is interested in flavor, not fire. Among the subtly seasoned offerings are *panang goong* (shrimp in curry-peanut sauce), chicken sautéed with ginger and pineapple, and flounder with a choice of four sauces. Mirrored walls and soft lights soften the ambience of this small downstairs dining room. ⊠ *2016 P St. NW,* ☎ *202/872–1144. AE, DC, MC, V.*

Georgetown/West End/Glover Park

Caribbean

$$–$$$$　✕ **Hibiscus Café.** African masks and multicolored neon ac-
★　cents hang from the ceiling of this mod restaurant, where weekend crowds are drawn by spicy jerk chicken, blackened fish, shrimp curry, and flavorful soups (try the butternut-ginger bisque). Perfectly fried calamari and a generous piece of shark in a pocket of fried bread are paired with ginger sauce or tangy pineapple chutney to make delectable starters. Desserts—banana mousse with rum sauce, coconut crème brulée—favor island fruits. The passion fruit punch is potent. ⊠ *3401 K St. NW,* ☎ *202/965–7170. AE, D, MC, V. No lunch. Closed Sun. and Mon.*

French

$$–$$$$　✕ **Bistro Français.** Washington's chefs head for Bistro Français for the minute steak maître d'hôtel or the sirloin with herb butter. Among amateur eaters the big draw is the rotisserie chicken. Daily specials may include *suprême* of salmon with broccoli mousse and beurre blanc. The restaurant is divided into two parts—the café side and the more formal dining room; the café menu includes sandwiches and omelets in addition to entrées. ⊠ *3128 M St. NW,* ☎ *202/ 338–3830. AE, DC, MC, V.*

$$–$$$$　✕ **La Chaumière.** A favorite of Washingtonians seeking an escape from the hurly-burly of Georgetown, La Chaumière has the rustic charm of a French country inn, particularly during the winter, when its central stone fireplace warms the room. Fish stew, mussels, and scallops are on the regular menu, and there are always several grilled fish specials. The restaurant also has a devoted following for its meat dishes, which include such hard-to-find entrées as venison. ⊠ *2813 M St. NW,* ☎ *202/338–1784. AE, DC, MC, V. Closed Sun. No lunch Sat.*

$$$ ✕ **Provence.** Lavish simplicity seems to be the key here, from
★   the amber-hued dining room decorated with terra-cotta tiles
and wire baskets holding dried flowers, to the fresh herbs
that flavor every entrée. For appetizers there might be a salad
of wild greens topped with roasted pigeon and cool foie gras
or a lightly broiled oyster gratin with a sauce you'll want
to dip your bread in. Lobster might be cooked in butter and
served with a bright red beet sauce, or prepared with white
truffle oil and parsley. The almond cake, buttery and warm,
with sorbet, ends the meal on a light but decadent note. ⊠
*2401 Pennsylvania Ave. NW, ☎ 202/296–1166. Reserva-
tions essential. AE, DC, MC, V. Closed Sun. No lunch Sat.*

Indonesian

$$ ✕ **Sarinah Satay House.** Dine in a lush, enclosed garden
★   with trees growing through the ceiling. Carved monkeys,
parrots, and puppets add to the setting, where batik-clad
waiters offer serenely unrushed service. The food at Sarinah Satay House is exquisite. Potato croquettes and the traditional *loempia* and *resoles* (crisp and soft spring rolls) come
with a tangy, chili-spiked peanut dipping sauce, while the
perfectly grilled chicken satay is accompanied by a smoky-
sweet peanut dip. At under $10, the combination *nasi
rames*—chicken in coconut sauce, beef skewers, and spicy
green beans with rice—is a bargain. ⊠ *1338 Wisconsin Ave.
NW, ☎ 202/337–2955. AE, D, DC, MC, V. Closed Mon.
No lunch Sun.*

Japanese

$$ ✕ **Sushi-Ko.** Sushi-Ko is the city's best Japanese restaurant.
★   Daily specials listed on a blackboard are always innovative:
Sesame-oil seasoned trout is layered with crisp wonton
crackers, and a sushi special might be salmon topped with
a touch of mango sauce and a tiny sprig of dill or thin
pieces of scallop with a touch of pesto sauce. And you won't
find their whimsical desserts like green tea mousse and sake
ice cream at the local bakeshop. ⊠ *2309 Wisconsin Ave.
NW, ☎ 202/333–4187. AE, MC, V. No lunch Sat.–Mon.*

New American

$$$$ ✕ **Citronelle.** The essence of California chic, Citronelle's
★   glass-front kitchen allows diners watch the chefs create
culinary masterpieces. A tart of thinly sliced, grilled scal-
lops might be served as an appetizer special. Loin of veni-

son might come with chestnuts, mushrooms, and wine sauce. Leek-encrusted salmon steak is topped by a crisp fried-potato lattice. Desserts are equally luscious: The crunchy napoleon—layers of caramelized phyllo dough between creamy vanilla custard—is drizzled with butterscotch and dark chocolate. ⊠ *3000 M St. NW,* ☎ *202/625–2150. AE, DC, MC, V.*

$$$–$$$$ ✕ **1789.** The elegant sage green dining room, with early
★   American paintings and a large fireplace, could easily be a room in the White House. But while the decor is proper and genteel, the food is down-to-earth and delicious. Soups, like the rich black bean soup seasoned with unsweetened chocolate and the plentiful seafood stew, are always surprising and flavorful. Rack of lamb and fillet of beef are specialties and seared tuna stands out among the excellent seafood dishes. Hazelnut chocolate bars with espresso sauce will pep you up for a night on the town, or opt for something homier like nectarine cobbler. ⊠ *1226 36th St. NW,* ☎ *202/965–1789. AE, D, DC, MC, V. No lunch.*

4 Lodging

By Jan
Ziegler

Updated
by CiCi
Williamson

ECAUSE WASHINGTON IS an international city, nearly all hotel staffs are multilingual. All hotels in the $$$ and $$$$ categories have concierges; some in the $$ group do, too. All the large hotels and many of the smaller ones offer meeting facilities and special features for business travelers. Nearly all the finer hotels have superb restaurants with high prices. Hostelries that provide breakfast are indicated by CP, which stands for Continental Plan. Most of the major chains have properties in desirable locations throughout town and in the nearby suburbs.

The hotel reviews here are grouped within neighborhoods according to price. Hotels' parking fees range from free (usually, but not always in the suburbs) to $22 a night. Street parking is not impossible, especially on weekends. During weekday rush hours, many streets are unavailable for parking. Read signs carefully; some are very confusing and the parking patrol is quick to ticket cars.

For a list of its member hotels, contact the **Washington, D.C., Convention and Visitors Association** (✉ 1212 New York Ave. NW, 20005, ☎ 202/789–7000).

To find reasonably priced accommodations in small guest houses and private homes, **Bed 'n' Breakfast Accommodations Ltd. of Washington, D.C.** (✉ Box 12011, 20005, ☎ 202/328–3510) is a good source.

CATEGORY	COST*
$$$$	over $190
$$$	$145–$190
$$	$100–$145
$	under $100

*All prices are for a standard double room, excluding room tax (13% in DC, 12% in MD, and 6.5 to 9.75% in VA) and $1.50 per night occupancy tax in D.C.

Capitol Hill

$$$–$$$$ 🏨 **Phoenix Park Hotel.** Named after a historic park in Dublin, the Phoenix Park has an Irish club theme and is

home to the Dubliner Pub, where Irish entertainers perform nightly. Across the street from Union Station and only four blocks from the Capitol, this hotel is popular with lobbyists, businesspeople, and tourists. The three penthouse suites have balconies overlooking Union Station. A renovation completed in March 1997 added more than 70 new guest rooms and a health club. ⊠ *520 N. Capitol St. NW, 20001,* ☎ *202/638–6900 or 800/824–5419,* FAX *202/393–3236. 150 rooms, 6 suites. Pub, in-room modem lines, laundry service, exercise room, parking (fee). AE, D, DC, MC, V. Metro: Union Station.*

$$$ 🏨 **Capitol Hill Suites.** On a quiet residential street behind the Library of Congress, this all-suite hotel's proximity to the House office buildings means that it is often filled with visiting lobbyists when Congress is in session. Guest rooms are large and the cozy, sun-filled lobby has a fireplace. ⊠ *200 C St. SE, 20003,* ☎ *202/543–6000 or 800/424–9165,* FAX *202/547–2608. 152 suites. Kitchens, parking (fee). AE, DC, MC, V. Metro: Capitol South.*

$$–$$$ 🏨 **Holiday Inn on the Hill.** For clean, comfortable, low-priced rooms with high-priced views, this is the place. This Holiday Inn offers the same magnificent views of the Capitol as the nearby Hyatt. Children under age 18 stay free. ⊠ *415 New Jersey Ave. NW, 20001,* ☎ *202/638–1616 or 800/638–1116,* FAX *202/638–0707. 338 rooms, 8 suites. Restaurant, bar, room service, pool, sauna, exercise room, parking (fee). AE, D, DC, MC, V. Metro: Union Station.*

Downtown

$$$$ 🏨 **Jefferson Hotel.** Federal-style elegance abounds inside
★ this small luxury hotel next door to the National Geographic Society and opposite the Russian Embassy. The 100 rooms and suites have antiques, original art, VCRs, and CD players; you may borrow from the hotel's video and CD libraries. The Dining Room restaurant, serving American cuisine, is a favorite among high-ranking politicos and film stars. A high staff-to-guest ratio ensures outstanding service: Employees greet you by name and laundry is hand ironed and delivered in wicker baskets. ⊠ *1200 16th St. NW, 20036,* ☎ *202/347–2200 or 800/368–5966,* FAX *202/785–1505. 68 rooms, 32 suites. Restaurant, bar, room*

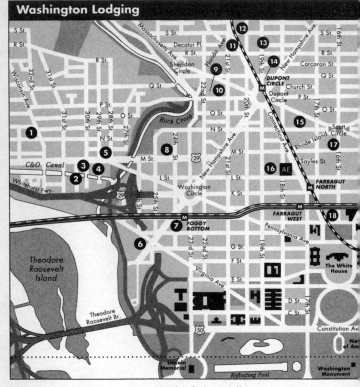

Washington Lodging

ANA Hotel, **8**

Capitol Hill Suites, **28**

Channel Inn, **25**

Doubletree Guest Suites, **7**

Dupont Plaza, **14**

Four Seasons Hotel, **5**

Georgetown Dutch Inn, **2**

Georgetown Inn, **1**

Georgetown Suites, **4**

Hay-Adams Hotel, **18**

Henley Park Hotel, **21**

Holiday Inn on the Hill, **27**

Hotel Harrington, **24**

Hotel Sofitel Washington, **11**

Hotel Tabard Inn, **15**

Hotel Washington, **22**

ITT Sheraton Luxury Collection Washington D.C., **10**

Jefferson Hotel, **17**

Latham Hotel, **3**

Lincoln Suites Downtown, **16**

Loews L'Enfant Plaza, **26**

Morrison-Clark Inn, **19**

Normandy Inn, **13**

Phoenix Park Hotel, **29**

Radisson Barceló Hotel, **9**

Washington International AYH-Hostel, **20**

Washington Hilton and Towers, **12**

Watergate Hotel, **6**

Willard Inter-Continental, **23**

service, in-room VCRs, laundry service, parking (fee). AE, DC, MC, V. Metro: Farragut North.

$$$$ ☆ **Willard Inter-Continental.** Just two blocks from the
★ White House, the Willard, whose present building dates from 1901, has welcomed every American president from Franklin Pierce in 1853 to Dwight Eisenhower in the 1950s, before closing after years of decline. The new Willard, a faithful renovation, is an opulent beaux arts feast for the eye: The main lobby has spectacular proportions, great columns, huge chandeliers, mosaic floors, and elaborately carved ceilings. The hotel's formal eatery, the Willard Room, has won nationwide acclaim. ⊠ *1401 Pennsylvania Ave. NW, 20004,* ☎ *202/628–9100 or 800/327–0200,* 𝖥𝖠𝖷 *202/637–7326. 340 rooms, 39 suites. 2 restaurants, 2 bars, minibars, room service, health club, laundry service and dry cleaning, meeting rooms, parking (fee). AE, DC, MC, V. Metro: Metro Center.*

$$$–$$$$ ☆ **Hay-Adams Hotel.** This Italian Renaissance landmark
★ is across Lafayette Park from the White House. Reserve a room on the south side well in advance to enjoy the city's best view of the mansion and Washington Monument beyond. The Hay-Adams has an eclectic grandeur inside: European and Oriental antiques; Doric, Ionic, and Corinthian touches; carved walnut wainscoting; and intricate ornamental ceilings. The Lafayette dining room serves "contemporary American" dishes. The hotel's afternoon tea is renowned. ⊠ *1 Lafayette Sq. NW, 20006,* ☎ *202/638–6600 or 800/424–5054,* 𝖥𝖠𝖷 *202/638–2716. 125 rooms, 18 suites. Restaurant, bar, room service, laundry service and dry cleaning, parking (fee). AE, DC, MC, V. Metro: Farragut West or Farragut North.*

$$$–$$$$ ☆ **Henley Park Hotel.** A Tudor-style building adorned with
★ 119 gargoyles, this National Historic Trust hotel has the cozy charm of an English country house. The main eatery, Coeur de Lion, has a leafy atrium, stained-glass windows, and an American menu. Complimentary amenities include hors d'oeuvres and jazz nightly in Marley's Lounge, weekday limousine service to any downtown destination from 7:30 to 9:30 AM, and 24-hour room service. The hotel is a long, eight-block walk to the Smithsonian museums. ⊠ *926 Massachusetts Ave. NW, 20001,* ☎ *202/638–5200 or 800/ 222–8474,* 𝖥𝖠𝖷 *202/638–6740. 79 rooms, 17 suites. Restau-*

rant, bar, in-room modem lines, minibars room service, parking (fee). AE, DC, MC, V. Metro: Metro Center or Gallery Place/Chinatown.

$$–$$$$ ⊡ **Hotel Washington.** Since opening in 1918, the Hotel
★ Washington has been known for its view. Washingtonians bring visitors to the outdoor rooftop bar—open May to October—for cocktails and a panorama that includes the White House grounds and Washington Monument. Now a National Landmark, the hotel sprang from the drawing boards of John Carrère and Thomas Hastings, who designed the New York Public Library. Suite 506 is where Elvis Presley stayed on his trips to D.C. ⊠ *515 15th St. NW, 20004,* ☎ *202/638–5900,* FAX *202/638–1594. 344 rooms, 16 suites. 2 restaurants, bar, deli, lobby lounge, room service, exercise room, laundry service and dry cleaning, business services, parking (fee). AE, DC, MC, V. Metro: Metro Center.*

$$–$$$ ⊡ **Lincoln Suites Downtown.** The Lincoln Suites (formerly Hotel Anthony), which has a tiny lobby and reasonable prices, also has very large guest rooms. The center-city hotel's all-suite rooms include either a kitchen or wet bar, refrigerator, and microwave. The friendly staff offers free freshly baked cookies and milk every evening. Other amenities include free passes to Bally's Health and Fitness Club and free weekend breakfasts. ⊠ *1823 L St. NW, 20036,* ☎ *202/223–4320 or 800/424–2970,* FAX *202/223–8546. 99 suites. Restaurant, room service. AE, DC, MC, V. Metro: Farragut North.*

$$–$$$ ⊡ **Morrison-Clark Inn.** This inn is a merger of two 1864
★ Victorian town houses that served as the Soldiers, Sailors, Marines and Airmen's Club for 57 years. Mamie Eisenhower and Jacqueline Kennedy volunteered time at the club. One house has a 1917 Chinese Chippendale porch; the antique-filled public rooms have marble fireplaces, bay windows, and porch access. Guest rooms have either neoclassic or French country furnishings. The inn's highly rated restaurant serves American cuisine with Southern and other regional influences. ⊠ *Massachusetts Ave. and 11th St. NW, 20001,* ☎ *202/898–1200 or 800/332–7898,* FAX *202/289–8576. 54 rooms. CP. Restaurant, minibars, room service, exercise room, laundry service and dry cleaning, parking (fee). AE, D, DC, MC, V. Metro: Metro Center or Gallery Place/Chinatown.*

$–$$ 🏨 **Hotel Harrington.** Just three blocks from the J. W. Marriott and Grand Hyatt, the Harrington is miles away in price. This is one of Washington's oldest hotels, without frills but with low prices and right in the center of everything. It is very popular with springtime high school bus tours and with families, who like the two-bedroom, two-bathroom suites. ✉ *436 11th St. NW, 20004,* ☎ *202/628–8140 or 800/424–8532,* FAX *202/347–3924. 236 rooms, 24 suites. Restaurant, cafeteria, pub, room service, barber shop, coin laundry, meeting rooms, parking (fee). AE, D, DC, MC, V. Metro: Metro Center.*

$ 🏨 **Washington International AYH-Hostel.** This well-kept place has clean dormitory rooms with bunk beds and a kitchen, laundry room, and living room. Single men and women are in separate rooms; families are given their own room if the hostel is not full. The hostel also sponsors tours, movies, and other programs. The maximum stay is 29 days. College-age travelers predominate, and July–September is the busiest period. ✉ *1009 11th St. NW, 20001,* ☎ *202/737–2333,* FAX *202/737–1508. 250 beds. Kitchen, shop, coin laundry. MC, V. Metro: Chinatown.*

Dupont Circle

$$$$ 🏨 **Hotel Sofitel Washington.** Directly across Connecticut
★ Avenue from the Hilton, this French-owned hotel has rooms with small work areas. The Trocadero Café serves three meals daily. ✉ *1914 Connecticut Ave. NW, 20009,* ☎ *202/797–2000 or 800/424–2464,* FAX *202/462–0944. 107 rooms, 37 suites. Restaurant, bar, room service, minibars, exercise room, laundry service and dry cleaning, parking (fee). AE, DC, MC, V. Metro: Dupont Circle.*

$$$$ 🏨 **ITT Sheraton Luxury Collection Washington, D.C.** The childhood home of Al Gore, this intimate hotel that was a Ritz-Carlton until August 1997 has an English hunt-club theme; rooms have views of Embassy Row or Georgetown and the National Cathedral. The intimate Jockey Club restaurant, with its half-timber ceilings, dark wood paneling, and red-check tablecloths, draws the crowned heads of Washington. The Fairfax Bar is a cozy spot for a drink beside the fire (with piano entertainment some evenings). Afternoon tea is most proper. The hotel had yet to be

named at press time. ⊠ *2100 Massachusetts Ave. NW, 20008,* ☎ *202/293–2100 or 800/325–3589,* FAX *202/466– 9867. 174 rooms, 32 suites. Restaurant, bar, minibars, room service, in-room VCRs, massage, sauna, golf privileges, exercise room, meeting rooms, parking (fee). AE, DC, MC, V. Metro: Dupont Circle.*

$$–$$$$ 🏨 **Dupont Plaza.** Actually *on* Dupont Circle, the Dupont Plaza is as close as you can get to this colorful neighborhood of art galleries, bookstores, coffeehouses, and embassies. Its large lounge with huge windows facing Dupont Circle is perfect for people watching. Rooms are equipped with all the comforts, including extensive free electronic gadgets, oversize tubs, and a wet bar with refrigerator. Complimentary passes to the nearby Washington Sports Club are provided. ⊠ *1500 New Hampshire Ave. NW, 20036,* ☎ *202/483–6000,* FAX *202/328–3265. 314 rooms. Restaurant, bar, lobby lounge, outdoor café, parking (fee). AE, D, DC, MC, V. Metro: Dupont Circle.*

$$–$$$$ 🏨 **Washington Hilton and Towers.** A busy convention hotel
★   with extensive meeting and banqueting rooms, the Washington Hilton has guest rooms that are compact and sterile but light-filled, and because the hotel is on a hill, each has some view of the Washington skyline. Shops and restaurants of Dupont Circle and the Adams-Morgan neighborhood are just a short walk away. There are extensive indoor and outdoor athletic facilities. ⊠ *1919 Connecticut Ave. NW, 20009,* ☎ *202/483–3000 or 800/445–8667,* FAX *202/ 265–8221. 1,062 rooms, 88 suites. 2 restaurants, 2 bars, outdoor café, in-room modem lines, room service, pool, parking (fee). AE, DC, MC, V. Metro: Dupont Circle.*

$–$$$ 🏨 **Radisson Barceló Hotel.** Convenient to Dupont Circle and Georgetown, the Barceló was once an apartment building and has large rooms that are especially good for families. The second-floor outdoor swimming pool has a lovely setting—a brick courtyard is enclosed by the walls of the hotel and the backs of a row of century-old town houses to the east. Spanish fare is served at the Gabriel Restaurant. ⊠ *2121 P St. NW, 20037,* ☎ *202/293–3100* FAX *202/857– 0134. 235 rooms, 65 suites. Restaurant, bar, tapas bar, room service, sauna, exercise room, parking (fee). AE, D, DC, MC, V. Metro: Dupont Circle.*

$ 🏨 **Hotel Tabard Inn.** Formed by a linkage of three Victorian town houses, the Hotel Tabard Inn is one of the oldest continuously running hostelries in D.C. Named after the inn in Chaucer's *Canterbury Tales,* it's furnished throughout with Victorian and American Empire antiques; the floors are creaky and the plumbing is old-fashioned. Dim lighting and a genteel shabbiness are off-putting to some and charming to others. The street is quiet, and Dupont Circle and the K Street business district are nearby. Passes are provided to the nearby YMCA, which has extensive fitness facilities. The Tabard's restaurant is popular with locals. ✉ *1739 N St. NW, 20036,* ☎ *202/785–1277,* 𝔽𝔸𝕏 *202/785– 6173. 40 rooms, 25 with bath. CP. Restaurant, lobby lounge. MC, V. Metro: Dupont Circle.*

Georgetown

$$$$ 🏨 **Four Seasons Hotel.** The Four Seasons Hotel may be a
★   modern brick-and-glass edifice amid Georgetown's 19th-century Federal and Georgian row houses, but inside Old World elegance prevails; the rich mahogany paneling, antiques, spectacular flower arrangements, and impeccable service are hallmarks of a mecca for Washington's elite. Views from guest rooms are: the C&O Canal, the trees and streams of Rock Creek Park, the busy Georgetown street scene, or the quiet courtyard. In mid-1998, the already extensive health club will be doubled in size and 40 suites will be added. ✉ *2800 Pennsylvania Ave. NW, 20007,* ☎ *202/ 342–0444 or 800/332–3442,* 𝔽𝔸𝕏 *202/342–1673. 167 rooms, 30 suites. 2 restaurants, bar, room service, pool, health club, nightclub, concierge, parking (fee). AE, DC, MC, V. Metro: Foggy Bottom.*

$$$–$$$$ 🏨 **Georgetown Inn.** With an atmosphere reminiscent of an old gentleman's sporting club, the redbrick Georgetown Inn is a quiet, intimate, European-style hotel with an 18th-century flavor. At its Georgetown Bar & Grill everyone from shorts-clad tourists to pin-striped businesspeople can feel at home. ✉ *1310 Wisconsin Ave. NW, 20007,* ☎ *202/333– 8900 or 800/424–2979,* 𝔽𝔸𝕏 *202/625–1744. 95 rooms, 8 suites. Restaurant, bar, in-room modem lines, room service, exercise room, parking (fee). AE, DC, MC, V. Metro: Foggy Bottom.*

Pick up the phone.
Pick up the miles.

1-800-FLY-FREE

Is this a great time, or what? :-)

Now when you sign up with MCI you can receive up to 8,000 bonus frequent flyer miles on one of seven major airlines.

Then earn another 5 miles for every dollar you spend on a variety of MCI services, including MCI Card® calls from virtually anywhere in the world.*

You're going to use these services anyway. Why not rack up the miles while you're doing it?

Urban planning.

CITYPACKS

The ultimate guide to the city—a complete pocket guide plus a full-size color map.

www.fodors.com

$$$–$$$$ 🏨 **Georgetown Suites.** If you consider standard hotel rooms cramped and overpriced, the Georgetown Suites—in a brick courtyard one block south of M Street in the heart of Georgetown—is a find. Suites vary in size but all have large kitchens, irons and ironing boards, hair dryers, and voice mail. Children under 12 stay free. ⊠ *1111 30th St. NW, 20007,* ☎ *202/298–7800 or 800/348–7203,* FAX *202/ 333–5792. 216 suites. CP. Kitchens, in-room modem lines, exercise room, laundry service and dry cleaning, parking (fee). AE, DC, MC, V. Metro: Foggy Bottom.*

$$$–$$$$ 🏨 **Latham Hotel.** This small Federal-style hotel on Georgetown's fashionable main avenue has immaculate, beautifully decorated guest rooms, many with treetop views of "George's town," the Potomac River, and the C&O Canal. The polished brass and glass lobby leads to Citronelle (☞ Chapter 3), which is among the city's best restaurants; a La Madeleine bakery/eatery is also on site. Three blocks away is Georgetown Park, a handsome, upscale shopping mall. ⊠ *3000 M St. NW, 20007,* ☎ *202/726–5000 or 800/ 368–5922,* FAX *202/337–4250. 143 rooms, 21 suites. 2 restaurants, bar, in-room modem lines, minibars, room service, pool, parking (fee). AE, DC, MC, V. Metro: Foggy Bottom.*

$$$ 🏨 **Georgetown Dutch Inn.** A half block off M Street, Georgetown's main thoroughfare, this modest, Georgian-style all-suite hotel has large guest rooms and kitchens, and sofa beds and dinette sets in the living rooms. Breakfast is served in the small lobby decorated with 18th-century touches. ⊠ *1075 Thomas Jefferson St. NW, 20007,* ☎ *202/337–0900,* FAX *202/333–6526. 47 suites. CP. Room service. AE, DC, MC, V. Metro: Foggy Bottom.*

Southwest

$$$–$$$$ 🏨 **Loews L'Enfant Plaza.** Just two blocks from Smithsonian museums, this hotel, which sits atop a shopping mall/office complex and Metro stop, has guest rooms with spectacular river, Capitol, or monument views. Its proximity to several government agencies (USDA, USPS, USIA, and DOT) makes it popular with business travelers. The American Grill restaurant serves—surprise—regional American food. ⊠ *L'Enfant Plaza SW, 20024,* ☎ *202/484–1000 or*

800/223–0888, ℻ 202/646–4456. *348 rooms, 22 suites.*
Restaurant, 2 bars, room service, minibars, in-room VCRs,
indoor pool, health club, parking (fee). AE, DC, MC, V.
Metro: L'Enfant Plaza.

$–$$ ⊞ **Channel Inn.** The only hotel on Washington's waterfront,
this property overlooks Washington Channel, the marina,
and the Potomac River. The hotel is home to the Pier 7
Restaurant and Engine Room Lounge. Public areas and meet-
ings rooms have a nautical motif with mahogany panels and
marine artifacts. The parking is free, a rarity in Washington. The Mall, Smithsonian, Treasury, and several other government offices are close. Access to a nearby health club is
free of charge. ⊠ *650 Water St. S.W., 20024,* ☎ *202/554–*
2400 or 800/368–5668, ℻ *202/863–1164. 100 rooms.*
Restaurant, bar, outdoor café, pool, meeting rooms, free
parking. AE, D, DC, MC, V. Metro: Waterfront.

Northwest/Upper Connecticut Avenue

$$ ⊞ **Normandy Inn.** A small, quaint European-style hotel on
★ a quiet street in the embassy area of Connecticut Avenue,
the Normandy is near fine dining and shopping. Rooms are
neat, cozy, and attractively decorated; all have refrigerators
and coffeemakers. Each Tuesday evening a wine-and-cheese
reception is held for guests. You can select a book from the
inn's library and read by the fireplace in the lobby while
enjoying the complimentary coffee and tea that is available
in the morning and afternoon. ⊠ *2118 Wyoming Ave.*
NW, 20008, ☎ *202/483–1350 or 800/424–3729,* ℻ *202/*
387–8241. 75 rooms. CP. Refrigerators, parking (fee). AE,
D, MC, V. Metro: Dupont Circle.

West End/Foggy Bottom

$$$$ ⊞ **ANA Hotel.** The Japanese-owned ANA Hotel is a stylish
★ combination of the contemporary and the traditional. The
beautiful glassed lobby and about a third of the bright, airy
rooms have views of the central courtyard and gardens,
which are popular for weddings. The hotel's informal
restaurant, the Bistro, has the flavor of 19th-century Paris
and contains an antique mahogany bar. The state-of-the-
art health club has a lap pool. ⊠ *2401 M St. NW, 20037,*

☎ *202/429–2400 or 800/228–3000,* FAX *202/457–5010.
406 rooms, 9 suites. 2 restaurants, bar, café, room service,
beauty salon, pool, health club, sauna, steam room, parking (fee). AE, DC, MC, V. Metro: Foggy Bottom.*

$$$$ ⊞ **Watergate Hotel.** The internationally famous Water-
★   gate is accustomed to serving the world's elite. The lobby
sets a genteel tone with its classic columns, Oriental rugs
on black and white checkerboard marble, subdued lighting, and soothing classical music. On the Potomac River,
the hotel is across the street from the Kennedy Center, and
a short walk from the State Department and Georgetown.
Originally intended as apartments, the guest rooms are
large, and all have walk-in closets and fax machines. The
hotel's riverside restaurant, Aquarelle, serves sophisticated
Euro-American cuisine. The Potomac Lounge and The
Crescent Bar are two favorite Washington meeting places
for a traditional afternoon tea or cocktails. There's complimentary limousine service weekdays 7 to 10 AM. ⊠
2650 Virginia Ave. NW, 20037, ☎ *202/965–2300 or 800/
424–2736,* FAX *202/337–7915. 90 rooms, 141 suites.
Restaurant, 2 bars, room service, indoor pool, health club,
parking (fee). AE, DC, MC, V. Metro: Foggy Bottom.*

$$–$$$ ⊞ **Doubletree Guest Suites.** In a quiet section of New
Hampshire Avenue, close to the Kennedy Center, the all-
suite Doubletree has accommodations with kitchens and
sofa sleepers as extra beds. The staff is small as is the lobby.
There is an outdoor rooftop pool (a great spot for viewing
fireworks on July 4). ⊠ *801 New Hampshire Ave. NW,
20037,* ☎ *202/785–2000 or 800/424–2900,* FAX *202/785–
9485. 224 suites. Kitchens, in-room modem lines, room service, coin laundry, dry cleaning, parking (fee). AE, DC, MC,
V. Metro: Foggy Bottom.*

5 Nightlife and the Arts

THE ARTS

By John F.
Kelly

Updated
by Robert
Reid-Pharr

In the past 20 years, Washington has been transformed into a cultural capital. The Kennedy Center is a world-class venue, home of the National Symphony Orchestra and host to Broadway shows, ballet, modern dance, opera, and more. Washington even has its own "off Broadway": a half dozen or so plucky theaters spread out around the city offer new twists on both old and new works. Several art galleries present highly regarded chamber music series. The service bands from the area's numerous military bases ensure an endless supply of martial music of the John Philip Sousa variety as well as rousing renditions of more contemporary tunes. Washington was the birthplace of hardcore, a socially aware form of punk rock music that has influenced young bands throughout the country. Go-go—infectious, rhythmic music mixing elements of rap, rhythm and blues, and funk—has been touted as the next big sound to go national but still seems confined largely to Washington.

Friday's *Washington Post* "Weekend" section is the best guide to events for the weekend and the coming week. The *Post*'s daily "Guide to the Lively Arts" also outlines cultural events in the city. The *Washington Times* "Weekend" section comes out on Thursday. The free weekly *Washington CityPaper* hits the streets on Thursday and covers the entertainment scene well. You might also consult the "City Lights" section in the monthly *Washingtonian* magazine.

Tickets

Protix takes reservations for events at Arena Stage, Center Stage, Ford's Theater, the Holocaust Museum, and Signature Theater. It also has outlets in selected Waxie Maxies. ☎ *703/218–6500.*

TicketMaster takes phone charges for events at most venues around the city. You can purchase TicketMaster tickets in person at all Hecht's department stores. No refunds or exchanges are allowed. ☎ *202/432–7328 or 800/551–7328.*

TicketPlace sells half-price, day-of-performance tickets for selected shows; a "menu board" lists available performances. Only cash is accepted, and there's a 10% service charge per order. TicketPlace also is a full-price TicketMaster outlet. ⊠ *Lisner Auditorium, 730 21st St. NW,* ☎ *202/842–5387.* ⊙ *Tues.–Fri. noon–6, Sat. 11–5. Tickets for Sun. and Mon. performances sold on Sat.*

Dance

Dance Place. A studio theater that presented its first performance in 1980, Dance Place hosts a wide assortment of modern and ethnic dance most weekends. ⊠ *3225 8th St. NE,* ☎ *202/269–1600.*

Smithsonian Associates Program (☞ Smithsonian Institution, *below*). National and international dance groups often perform at various Smithsonian museums. ☎ *202/ 357–3030.*

Washington Ballet. Between September and May this company presents classical and contemporary ballets from the works of such choreographers as George Balanchine, Marius Petipa, and Choo-San Goh at the Kennedy Center and the Warner Theatre. ☎ *202/362–3606.*

Film

American Film Institute. More than 700 different movies—including contemporary and classic foreign and American films—are shown each year at the American Film Institute's theater in the Kennedy Center. Filmmakers and actors are often present to discuss their work. ⊠ *Kennedy Center, New Hampshire Ave. and Rock Creek Pkwy. NW,* ☎ *202/785–4600.*

Hirshhorn Museum. For avant-garde and experimental film lovers, weekly movies—often first-run documentaries, features, and short films—are shown free. ⊠ *8th and Independence Ave. SW,* ☎ *202/357–2700.*

National Archives. Historical films are shown on a daily basis. Check the calendar of events for movie listings. ⊠ *8th and Constitution Aves. NW,* ☎ *202/501–5000.*

National Gallery of Art East Building. Free classic and international films that are usually complementary to exhibits are shown in this museum's large auditorium. Pick up a film calendar at the museum for movie listings. ⊠ *4th and Constitution NW,* ☎ *202/737–4215.*

National Geographic Society. Educational films with a scientific, geographic, or anthropological focus are shown here weekly. ⊠ *17th and M Sts. NW,* ☎ *202/857–7588.*

Music

Chamber Music
Corcoran Gallery of Art. Hungary's Takacs String Quartet and the Cleveland Quartet are among the chamber groups that appear in the Corcoran's Musical Evening Series, one Friday each month from October to May, with some summer offerings. Concerts are followed by a reception with the artists. ⊠ *17th St. and New York Ave. NW,* ☎ *202/639-1700.*

Folger Shakespeare Library. The Folger Shakespeare Library's internationally acclaimed resident chamber music ensemble, the Folger Consort, regularly presents a selection of instrumental and vocal pieces from the medieval, Renaissance, and Baroque periods, during a season that runs from October to May. ⊠ *201 E. Capitol St. SE,* ☎ *202/544–7077.*

National Academy of Sciences. Free performances are given October through May in the academy's acoustically nearly perfect 670-seat auditorium. Both the National Musical Arts Chamber Ensemble and the United States Marines Chamber Orchestra perform regularly. ⊠ *2101 Constitution Ave. NW,* ☎ *202/334–2436.*

Phillips Collection. Duncan Phillips's mansion is more than an art museum. From September through May the long paneled music room hosts Sunday afternoon recitals. Chamber groups from around the world perform; May is devoted to performing artists from the Washington area. Concerts begin at 5 PM, but arrive early for decent seats. ⊠ *1600 21st St. NW,* ☎ *202/387–2151.*

Choral Music
Basilica of the National Shrine of the Immaculate Conception. Choral and church groups frequently perform in this

impressive venue. ✉ *Michigan Ave. and 4th St. NE,* ☎ *202/526–8300.*

Choral Arts Society of Washington. The 180-voice Choral Arts Society choir performs a varied selection of classical pieces at the Kennedy Center from September to June. Three Christmas sing-alongs are scheduled each December. ✉ *New Hampshire Ave. and Rock Creek Pkwy. NW,* ☎ *202/244–3669.*

Washington National Cathedral. Choral and church groups frequently perform in this grand cathedral. ✉ *Wisconsin and Massachusetts Aves. NW,* ☎ *202/537–6200.*

Concert Halls

DAR Constitution Hall. The 3,700-seat Constitution Hall hosts visiting performers, from jazz to pop to rap. ✉ *18th and C Sts. NW,* ☎ *202/628–4780.*

John F. Kennedy Center for the Performing Arts. Any search for cultured entertainment should start at the John F. Kennedy Center for the Performing Arts. The "KenCen" has a little of everything. It is actually five stages under one roof: the **Concert Hall,** home park of the National Symphony Orchestra; the 2,200-seat **Opera House,** the setting for ballet, modern dance, opera, and large-scale musicals; the **Eisenhower Theater,** usually used for drama; the **Terrace Theater,** a Philip Johnson–designed space that showcases chamber groups and experimental works; and the **Theater Lab,** home to cabaret-style performances (since 1987 the audience-participation hit mystery, **Shear Madness,** has been playing here). ✉ *New Hampshire Ave. and Rock Creek Pkwy. NW,* ☎ *202/467–4600 or 800/444–1324.*

Lisner Auditorium. A 1,500-seat theater on the campus of George Washington University, Lisner Auditorium is the setting for pop, classical, and choral music. ✉ *21st and H Sts. NW,* ☎ *202/994–6800.*

National Gallery of Art. Free concerts by the National Gallery Orchestra, conducted by George Manos, plus performances by outside recitalists and ensembles, are held in the venerable West Building's West Garden Court on Sunday evenings from October to June. Most performances highlight classical music, though April's American Music Festival often features jazz. Entry is first-come, first-served. ⊠ *6th St. and Constitution Ave. NW,* ☎ *202/842–6941 or 202/842–6698.*

Smithsonian Institution. A rich assortment of music—both free and ticketed—is presented by the Smithsonian. American jazz, musical theater, and popular standards are performed in the National Museum of American History. In the third-floor Hall of Musical Instruments, musicians periodically perform on historic instruments from the museum's collection. The **Smithsonian Associates Program** (☎ 202/357–3030) offers everything from a cappella groups to Cajun zydeco bands. ⊠ *1000 Jefferson Dr. SW,* ☎ *202/357–2700.*

US Airways Arena. The home stadium for the Washington Capitals hockey and Washington Bullets basketball teams is also the area's top venue for big-name pop, rock, and rap acts. Formerly known as the Capital Centre, it seats 20,000. ⊠ *1 Harry S. Truman Dr., Landover, MD,* ☎ *301/350–3400 or 202/432–7328.*

Orchestra

National Symphony Orchestra. The season at the Kennedy Center extends from September to June. One of the cheapest ways to hear—if not necessarily see—the NSO perform in the Kennedy Center Concert Hall is to get a $10 obstructed view ticket. ⊠ *New Hampshire Ave. and Rock Creek Pkwy NW,* ☎ *202/416–8100.*

Performance Series

Carter Barron Amphitheater. On Saturday and Sunday nights from mid-June to August this lovely, 4,250-seat outdoor theater in Rock Creek Park hosts pop, jazz, gospel, and rhythm and blues artists such as Chick Corea, Nancy Wilson, and Tito Puente. The National Symphony Orchestra also performs, and for two weeks in June the Shakespeare Theatre presents a free play by the Bard. ⊠ *16th St. and Colorado Ave. NW,* ☎ *202/426–6837; off-season,* ☎ *202/426–0486.*

District Curators. An independent, nonprofit organization, the District Curators group presents adventurous contemporary performers from around the world in spaces around the city, mostly in summer (June–August). Much of their season is encompassed by their Jazz Arts Festival. Past artists have included Laurie Anderson, Philip Glass, the

World Saxophone Quartet, and the Japanese dance troupe Sankai Juku. ☎ *202/783–0360.*

Ft. Dupont Summer Theater. When it comes to music in Washington, even the National Park Service gets in on the act. NPS presents national and international jazz artists at 8:30 on Friday and Saturday evenings from mid-June to August at the outdoor Ft. Dupont Summer Theater. Wynton Marsalis, Betty Carter, and Ramsey Lewis are among the artists who have performed free concerts. ⊠ *Minnesota Ave. and F St. SE,* ☎ *202/426–7723 or 202/619–7222.*

Sylvan Theater. Service bands from the army, air force, and marines perform alfresco at the Sylvan Theater from mid-June to August, Tuesday, Thursday, Friday, and Sunday nights at 8PM. ⊠ *Washington Monument grounds,* ☎ *202/619–7222.*

Opera

Washington Opera. Seven operas—presented in their original languages with English supertitles—are performed each season (November–March) in the Kennedy Center's Opera House and Eisenhower Theater. Performances are often sold out to subscribers, but returned tickets can be purchased an hour before curtain time. Standing room tickets go on sale at the Kennedy Center box office each Saturday at 10 AM for the following week's performances. ⊠ *New Hampshire Ave. and Rock Creek Pkwy. NW,* ☎ *202/416–7800 or 800/876–7372.*

Theater

Commercial Theaters and Companies

Arena Stage. The city's most respected resident company (established 1950), the Arena was the first theater outside New York to win a Tony award. It presents a wide-ranging season in its three theaters: the Fichandler Stage, the proscenium Kreeger, and the cabaret-style Old Vat Room. ⊠ *6th St. and Maine Ave. SW,* ☎ *202/488–3300.*

Ford's Theatre. Looking much as it did when President Lincoln was shot at a performance of *Our American Cousin,*

Ford's is host to both plays and musicals, many with family appeal. ⊠ *511 10th St. NW,* ☎ *202/347–4833.*

Lincoln Theatre. From the 1920s to the 1940s, the Lincoln hosted the same performers as the Cotton Club and the Apollo Theatre in New York City: Cab Calloway, Lena Horne, Duke Ellington. The 1,250-seater shows films and welcomes such acts as the Count Basie Orchestra and the Harlem Boys and Girls Choir. ⊠ *1215 U St. NW,* ☎ *202/ 328–6000.*

National Theatre. Destroyed by fire and rebuilt four times, the National Theatre has operated in the same location since 1835. It presents pre- and post-Broadway shows. ⊠ *1321 E St. NW,* ☎ *202/628–6161.*

Shakespeare Theatre. Four plays—three by the Bard, another a classic from his era—are staged each year by the acclaimed Shakespeare Theatre troupe. The troupe performs in a state-of-the-art, 447-seat space. For two weeks each June the company has its own version of New York's Shakespeare in the Park: a free play under the stars at Carter Barron Amphitheatre (☞ *above*). ⊠ *450 7th St. NW,* ☎ *202/393–2700.*

Warner Theatre. One of Washington's grand theaters, this 1924 building hosts road shows, dance recitals, and the occasional pop music act. ⊠ *13th and E Sts. NW,* ☎ *202/ 783–4000.*

Small Theaters and Companies
Gala Hispanic Theatre. The company produces Spanish classics as well as contemporary and modern Latin American plays in both Spanish and English. ⊠ *1625 Park Rd. NW,* ☎ *202/234–7174.*

Source Theatre. The 107-seat Source Theatre presents established plays with a sharp satirical edge and modern interpretations of classics. Each July and August, Source hosts the Washington Theater Festival, a series of performances of new plays, many by local playwrights. ⊠ *1835 14th St. NW,* ☎ *202/462–1073.*

Studio Theatre. An eclectic season of classic and offbeat plays is presented by one of the best of Washington's small, independent companies. ⊠ *1333 P St. NW,* ☎ *202/332–3300.*

Washington Stage Guild. Washington Stage Guild performs the classics as well as more contemporary fare in historic Carroll Hall. Shaw is a specialty. ⊠ *924 G St. NW,* ☎ *202/529–2084.*

Woolly Mammoth. Unusual, imaginatively produced shows have earned Woolly Mammoth good reviews and favorable comparisons to Chicago's Steppenwolf. ⊠ *1401 Church St. NW,* ☎ *202/393–3939.*

NIGHTLIFE

Even though the after-dark scene has contracted a bit in the last few years, Washington's nightlife still offers an array of watering holes, comedy clubs, discos, and intimate musical venues catering to a wide spectrum of customers, from proper political appointees to blue-collar regulars in from the suburbs. Many nightspots are clustered in a few key areas. Georgetown leads the pack with an explosion of bars, nightclubs, and restaurants on M Street east and west of Wisconsin Avenue and on Wisconsin Avenue north of M Street. A half dozen Capitol Hill bars can be found on a stretch of Pennsylvania Avenue between 2nd and 4th streets SE. There is another high-density nightlife area around the intersection of 19th and M streets NW, near the city's lawyer- and lobbyist-filled downtown.

To find out what's going on in Washington, consult Friday's "Weekend" section in the *Washington Post* and the free weekly *Washington CityPaper.* It's also a good idea to call clubs ahead of time to find out who's on that night and what sort of music will be played. Reservations are advised for cabaret shows and comedy clubs; we note where reservations are essential.

Acoustic/Folk/Country Clubs

For information on different folk events, call the recorded information line of the **Folklore Society of Greater Washington** (☎ 202/546–2228).

Afterwords. Shoehorned in the Kramerbooks store, near Dupont Circle, folkish acts entertain browsing bohemian bookworms as well as patrons seated at a cozy in-store café. ⊠ *1517 Connecticut Ave. NW,* ☎ *202/387–1462.* ⊘ *Mon.–Thurs. 7:30 AM–1 AM, Fri.–Mon. 7:30 AM–1 AM.*

Birchmere. Audiences come to listen to acoustic folk and bluegrass acts, and the management politely insists on no distracting chatter. ⊠ *3701 Mt. Vernon Ave., Alexandria, VA,* ☎ *703/549–5919. MC, V.* ⊘ *Sun.–Thurs. 6:30 PM– 11 PM, Fri. and Sat. 7 PM–12:30 AM.*

Junction. Local country-and-western fans consider this one of the best places to learn the two-step, and then practice it. ⊠ *1330 E. Gude Dr., Rockville, MD,* ☎ *301/217– 5820. AE, D, MC, V.* ▨ *Cover charge Fri. and Sat.* ⊘ *Fri.– Sun. 11 AM–2 AM, Tues.–Thurs. 11 AM–1 AM.*

Bars and Lounges

Brickskeller. A beer lover's mecca, this is the place to go when you want something more exotic than a Bud Lite. More than 800 brands of beer are for sale—from Central American lagers to U.S. microbrewed ales. ⊠ *1523 22nd St. NW,* ☎ *202/293–1885.* ⊘ *Mon.–Thurs. 11:30 AM–2 AM, Fri. 11:30 AM–3 AM, Sat. 6 PM–3 AM, Sun. 6 PM–2 AM.*

Capital City Brewing Company. In the New York Avenue location of this microbrewery, a gleaming copper bar dominates the scene, while metal steps lead up to where the brews are actually made. Their fabulous Postal Square site on Massachusetts Avenue has five thirty-keg copper serving vessels and a gorgeous vault door opening to the mezzanine left over from the days when the building was a functioning post office. ⊠ *1100 New York Ave. NW,* ☎ *202/628– 2222; 2 Massachusetts Ave. NE,* ☎ *202/842–2337.* ⊘ *Mon.–Sat. 11 AM–2 AM, Sun. 11 AM–midnight.*

Champions. With the evening's big game on the big-screen TV and the walls covered with jerseys, pucks, bats, and balls, this popular Georgetown establishment is a sports lover's oasis. Ballpark-style food enhances the mood. ⊠ *1206 Wisconsin Ave. NW,* ☎ *202/965–4005.* ⊘ *Mon.–Thurs. 5 PM–2 AM, Fri. 5 PM–3 AM, Sat. 11:30 AM–3 AM, Sun. 11:30 AM–2 AM. 1-drink minimum Fri. and Sat. after 10 PM.*

Dubliner. Snug paneled rooms, thick Guinness, and nightly live entertainment make Washington's premier Irish pub popular among Capitol Hill staffers. ⊠ *520 N. Capitol St. NW,* ☎ *202/737–3773.* ⊘ *Sun.–Thurs. 11 AM–1:30 AM, Fri.–Sat. 11 AM–2:30 AM.*

Food for Thought. Lots of Birkenstock sandals, and activist conversation give this Dupont Circle lounge and restaurant (vegetarian and organic meat) a '60s coffeehouse feel. Nightly folk music completes the picture. ⊠ *1738 Connecticut Ave. NW,* ☎ *202/797–1095.* ⊘ *Mon.–Thurs. 11:30 AM–12:30 AM (closed Mon. 3–5), Fri. 11:30 AM–1:30 AM, Sat. noon–1:30 AM, Sun. 4 PM–12:30 AM.*

Sign of the Whale. The best hamburger in town is available at the bar of this well-known post-preppie/neo-yuppie haven. ⊠ *1825 M St. NW,* ☎ *202/785–1110.* ⊘ *Sun.–Thurs. 11 AM–2 AM, Fri. and Sat. 11 AM–3 AM.*

Cabaret

Capitol Steps. The musical political satire of the Capitol Steps, a group of current and former Hill staffers, is presented on Friday and Saturday at Chelsea's (☞ Dance Clubs, *below*), a Georgetown nightclub, and occasionally at other spots around town. ⊠ *1055 Thomas Jefferson St. NW; Chelsea's,* ☎ *202/298–8222; Capitol Steps, 703/683–8330.* ▣ *Cover charge.* ⊘ *Fri. at 8 and Sat. at 7:30 most weeks. Reservations essential.*

Gross National Product. After years of spoofing Republican administrations with such shows as *BushCapades* and *Man Without a Contra,* then aiming its barbs at the Democrats in *Clintoons,* the irreverent comedy troupe Gross National Product was most recently performing *Hell to the Chief.* GNP stages its shows at the Bayou in Georgetown. ☎ *202/783–7212 (GNP) for location and reservations.* ▣ *Ticket charge.* ⊘ *Shows Sat. 7:30 PM.*

Comedy Clubs

Garvin's Comedy Clubs. Garvin's, which pioneered the practice of organizing comedy nights in suburban hotels, is one of the oldest names in comedy in Washington. ✉ *West-park Hotel, 8401 Westpark Dr., Tysons Corner, VA;* ✉ *Augie's Restaurant, I-395 and S. Glebe Rd., Arlington, VA,* ☎ *202/872-8880.* 🎫 *Cover charge and drink minimum.* ⊘ *Westpark Fri. at 9, Sat. 8 and 10; Augie's Fri. and Sat. at 9. Reservations essential.*

Headliners. Intimate rooms in two suburban hotels are host to local and regional acts on weekdays and national talent on the weekends. ✉ *Holiday Inn, 2460 Eisenhower Ave., Alexandria, VA,* ☎ *703/379-4242.* ⊘ *Fri. at 9, Sat. 8:30 and 10:30;* ✉ *Holiday Inn, 8120 Wisconsin Ave., Bethesda, MD,* ☎ *301/942-4242.* ⊘ *Tues.-Thurs. at 8:30, Fri. and Sat. 8:30 and 10:30.* 🎫 *Cover charge. Reservations essential.*

Improv. A heavyweight on the Washington comedy scene, the Improv is descended from the club that sparked the stand-up boomlet in New York City and across the country. Name headliners are common. ✉ *1140 Connecticut Ave. NW,* ☎ *202/296-7008.* 🎫 *Cover charge and 2-item (not necessarily drinks) minimum.* ⊘ *Sun.-Thurs. at 8:30, Fri. and Sat. 8:30 and 10:30.*

Dance Clubs

Chelsea's. An elegant Georgetown club near the C&O Canal, Chelsea's has Ethiopian music on Monday; Arabic tunes on Wednesday; hot Latin acts Friday and Saturday; and Persian music on Sunday. ✉ *1055 Thomas Jefferson St. NW,* ☎ *202/298-8222.* 🎫 *Cover charge Fri. and Sat.* ⊘ *Wed., Thurs., and Sun. 9:30 PM-2 AM, Fri. and Sat. 9:30 PM-4 AM.*

The Edge. A huge dance club the size of half a city block, The Edge has a friendly, hip atmosphere. Different nights have different themes and crowds; call for information. With four dance floors and five sound systems, the action here never stops. ✉ *56 L St. SE,* ☎ *202/488-1200.* 🎫 *Cover charge.* ⊘ *Nightly; hrs vary.*

Tracks 2000. A gay club with a large contingent of straight regulars, this warehouse-district disco has one of the largest dance floors in town and stays open late. ✉ *1111 1st St.*

SE, ☎ 202/488–3320. ▣ *Cover charge.* ☉ *Thurs. 9 PM–4 AM, Fri. 9 PM–5 AM, Sat. 8 PM–6 AM, Sun. 4 PM–9:30 PM (tea dance) and 9:30 PM–4 AM.*

Zei. Zei (pronounced zee) is a New York–style dance club in a former electric power substation. It wants to attract "young, upscale, politically aware women and men" with the relentless thump of Euro-pop dance music and a design that includes a wall of television sets peering down on the proceedings. ✉ *1415 Zei Alley NW, 14th St. between H and I Sts. NW,* ☎ *202/842–2445. No tennis shoes.* ▣ *Cover charge.* ☉ *Wed. and Thurs. 10 PM–2 AM, Fri. and Sat. 10 PM–3 AM (call for occasional weeknight events).*

Jazz Clubs

Blues Alley. The restaurant turns out Creole cooking, while cooking on stage are such nationally known performers as Charlie Byrd and Ramsey Lewis. You can come for just the show, but those who come for a meal get better seats. ✉ *Rear 1073 Wisconsin Ave. NW,* ☎ *202/337–4141.* ▣ *Cover charge and $7 food/drink minimum.* ☉ *Sun.–Thurs. 6 PM–midnight, Fri. and Sat. 6 PM–2 AM. Shows at 8 and 10, plus occasional midnight shows Fri. and Sat.*

Café Lautrec. The Toulouse-Lautrec decor, French food, and Gallic atmosphere are almost enough to convince you you're on the Left Bank of the Seine rather than the right bank of the Potomac. Jazz is on nightly, with tap-dancing fixture Johne Forges hoofing atop tables most Fridays and Saturdays. ✉ *2431 18th St. NW,* ☎ *202/265–6436.* ▣ *$6 minimum Tues. and Thurs.–Sun.* ☉ *Sun.–Thurs. 5 PM–2 AM, Fri. and Sat. 5 PM–3 AM.*

One Step Down. Low-ceilinged, intimate, and boasting the best jazz jukebox in town, this small club books talented local artists and the occasional national act. The venue of choice for many New York jazz masters, the place is frayed and smoky, as a jazz club should be. Live music is presented Thursday–Monday. ✉ *2517 Pennsylvania Ave. NW,* ☎ *202/331–8863.* ▣ *Cover charge and minimum.* ☉ *Mon.–Thurs. 10 AM–2 AM, Fri. 10 AM–3 AM, Sat. noon–3 AM, Sun. noon–2 AM.*

Rock, Pop, and Rhythm and Blues Clubs

Bayou. In Georgetown, underneath the Whitehurst Free-way, the Bayou is a Washington fixture that showcases na-tional acts on weeknights and local talent on weekends. Tickets are available at the door or through TicketMaster. ⊠ *3135 K St. NW,* ☎ *202/333–2897.* ▨ *Cover charge.* ☽ *Generally open daily 8 PM–2 AM.*

Capitol Ballroom. One of the largest venues for alternative and rock music in Washington, the Capitol Ballroom holds 1,000 people and brings in such bands as Ministry, Iggy Pop, and Bad Religion. Depending on the act, tickets are avail-able at TicketMaster or the door. ⊠ *1015 Half St. SE,* ☎ *202/554–1500.* ▨ *Cover charge.* ☽ *Hrs vary according to show but generally open at 7:00 PM nightly. Dance club opens at 10:00 PM.*

Grog and Tankard. A college-age crowd downs cheap pitch-ers of beer while listening to exuberant local bands in the Grog and Tankard, a small, comfortably disheveled nightspot. ⊠ *2408 Wisconsin Ave. NW,* ☎ *202/333–3114.* ▨ *Cover charge after 9 PM.* ☽ *Sun.–Thurs. 5 PM–2 AM, Fri.–Sat. 5 PM–3 AM.*

6 Shopping

By
Deborah
Papier

Updated
by Bruce
Walker

IN RECENT YEARS, the city's shopping scene has been revitalized. Although some long-time retailers have gone bankrupt, Filene's Basement (the Boston-based upscale fashion discounter) has moved in to fill the gap left by Raleighs' departure, and the remaining department stores have upgraded both their facilities and their merchandise. Many of the smaller one-of-a-kind shops have managed to survive urban renewal, designer boutiques are increasing, and interesting specialty shops and minimalls are popping up all over town. Store hours vary greatly. Play it safe; call ahead. In general, Georgetown stores are open late and on Sunday; stores downtown that cater to office workers close at 6 PM and may not be open at all on Saturday or Sunday. Some stores extend their hours on Thursday. We list the shops' nearest Metro stations, but some shops might be a 15- to 20-minute walk from the Metro; we do not list Metro stops for the few stores that have no Metro within walking distance.

Sales tax is 6%; major credit cards are accepted virtually everywhere.

Shopping Districts

Adams-Morgan. Scattered among the dozens of Latin, Ethiopian, and Caribbean restaurants in this most bohemian of Washington neighborhoods are a score of the city's most eccentric shops. If quality is what you seek, it's a minefield; tread cautiously. Still, for the bargain hunter it's great fun. A word of caution—call ahead to verify hours. ⊠ *18th St. NW between Columbia Rd. and California Ave. Metro: Woodley Park.*

Dupont Circle. You might call Dupont Circle a working-class version of Georgetown—blue collar instead of blue blood, not as well kept, with more apartment buildings than houses. But make no mistake: This is one of Washington's most vibrant neighborhoods, and its many restaurants, offbeat shops, and specialty book and record stores lend it a distinctive, cosmopolitan air. ⊠ *Connecticut Ave. between M and S Sts. Metro: Dupont Circle.*

Eastern Market. As the Capitol Hill area has become gentrified, unique shops and boutiques have sprung up. Many are clustered around the 1873 building known as Eastern Market. Inside are produce and meat counters, plus the Market Five art gallery; outside are a farmer's market (on Saturdays) and a flea market (on weekends). ⊠ *7th and C Sts. SE. Metro: Eastern Market.*

Georgetown. Georgetown remains Washington's favorite shopping area. Though Georgetown is not on a subway line, and parking is impossible, people still flock here. The attraction (aside from the lively street scene) is the profusion of specialty shops in a charming, historic neighborhood. In addition to tony antiques, elegant crafts, and high-style shoe and clothing boutiques, the area offers books, music, and wares from popular chain stores like the Gap and Benetton. ⊠ *Intersection of Wisconsin Ave. and M St.; most stores lie to the east and west on M St., and to the north on Wisconsin. Metro: Foggy Bottom.*

Wisconsin Avenue. A major shopping district is on upper Wisconsin Avenue straddling the Maryland border. The Mazza Gallerie (☞ Malls and Outlets, *below*) mall is here and other department stores, such as Lord & Taylor and Saks Fifth Avenue (☞ Department Stores, *below*), are close by. ⊠ *Wisconsin Ave. between Jennifer St. NW and Western Ave. Metro: Friendship Heights.*

Department Stores

Filene's Basement. At this mecca for bargain hunters, steep discounts can be had on Christian Dior, Hugo Boss, Burberrys, and other designer labels. Off-price shoes, perfume, and accessories are offered as well. ⊠ *1133 Connecticut Ave. NW,* ☎ *202/872–8430. Metro: Farragut North;* ⊠ *5300 Wisconsin Ave. NW,* ☎ *202/966–0208. Metro: Friendship Heights.*

Hecht's. As a clothing/department store Hecht's is roughly comparable to Macy's. The clothes sold here are a mix of conservative and trendy lines, with the men's department assuming increasing importance. Cosmetics, lingerie, and housewares are also strong departments. ⊠ *12th and G Sts. NW,* ☎ *202/628–6661. Metro: Metro Center*

Lord & Taylor. Lord & Taylor lets the competition be all things to all people while it focuses on nonutilitarian housewares and classic clothing by such designers as Anne Klein and Ralph Lauren. All clothing is designed and made in the United States. ⊠ *5255 Western Ave. NW,* ☎ *202/362–9600. Metro: Friendship Heights.*

Neiman Marcus. If price is an object, this is definitely not the place to shop, although it's still fun to browse. The carefully selected merchandise includes couture clothes, furs, precious jewelry, crystal, and silver. ⊠ *Mazza Gallerie, 5300 Wisconsin Ave. NW,* ☎ *202/966–9700. Metro: Friendship Heights.*

Saks Fifth Avenue. Though not technically a Washington department store because it is just over the Maryland line, Saks is nonetheless a Washington institution. It has a wide selection of European and American couture clothes; other attractions are the shoe, jewelry, fur, and lingerie departments. ⊠ *5555 Wisconsin Ave.,* ☎ *301/657–9000. Metro: Friendship Heights.*

Malls and Outlets

Chevy Chase Pavilion. Across from Mazza Gallerie (☞ *below*) is the newer, similarly upscale Chevy Chase Pavilion. Its exclusive women's clothing stores include Joan & David and Steilmann European Selection (which carries Karl Lagerfeld's sportier KL line). Other specialty shops of note here are the Pottery Barn and Country Road Australia. ⊠ *5335 Wisconsin Ave. NW,* ☎ *202/686–5335. Metro: Friendship Heights.*

Mazza Gallerie. The Mazza Gallerie, a four-level mall, is anchored by the ritzy Neiman Marcus department store and the discount department store Filene's Basement. Other stores include Williams-Sonoma's kitchenware and Laura Ashley Home. ⊠ *5300 Wisconsin Ave. NW,* ☎ *202/966–6114. Metro: Friendship Heights.*

Old Post Office Pavilion. The city is justly proud of its Old Post Office Pavilion, a handsome shopping center in a historic building with 19th-century origins. In addition to a dozen food vendors, there are 17 shops, among them Condor Imports (for South American and African clothing and crafts) and Juggling Capitol (for beginner to expert jugglers). ⊠ *12th St. NW and Pennsylvania Ave.,* ☎ *202/289–4224. Metro: Federal Triangle.*

Shops at Georgetown Park. Near the hub of the Georgetown shopping district at the intersection of Wisconsin Avenue and M Street is Georgetown Park, a three-level mall that looks like a Victorian ice-cream parlor inside. The pricey clothing and accessory boutiques and ubiquitous chain stores (such as Victoria's Secret) draw tourists in droves. ⊠ *3222 M St. NW,* ☎ *202/298–5577. Metro: Foggy Bottom.*

Tysons Corner Center. This mall houses 240 retailers, including Bloomingdale's and Nordstrom. Next door to Tysons Corner, the **Galleria at Tysons II** (⊠ 2001 International Dr.) has 125 retailers, including Saks Fifth Avenue and Neiman Marcus. ⊠ *1961 Chain Bridge Rd.,* ☎ *703/ 893–9400.*

Specialty Stores

Antiques and Collectibles

Chenonceau Antiques. The mostly American 19th- and 20th-century pieces on these two floors were selected by a buyer with an exquisite eye. Merchandise includes beautiful 19th-century paisley scarves from India and from Scotland, and 1920s glass lamps. ⊠ *2314 18th St. NW,* ☎ *202/ 667–1651.* ☉ *Sat.–Sun.*

Cherishables. American 18th- and 19th-century furniture and decorative arts are the featured attractions at Cherishables; the emphasis is on the Federal period. ⊠ *1608 20th St. NW,* ☎ *202/785–4087. Metro: Dupont Circle.*

Georgetown Antiques Center. The center, in a Victorian town house, has two dealers who share space: **Cherub Gallery** (☎ 202/337–2224) specializes in Art Nouveau and Art Deco, and **Michael Getz Antiques** (☎ 202/338–3811) sells fireplace equipment and silverware. ⊠ *2918 M St. NW. Metro: Foggy Bottom.*

Marston Luce. Focusing on American folk art, including quilts, weather vanes, and hooked rugs, Marston Luce also carries home and garden furnishings, primarily American, but some English and French as well. ⊠ *1314 21st St. NW,* ☎ *202/775–9460. Metro: Dupont Circle.*

Miller & Arney Antiques. English, American, and European furniture and accessories from the 18th and early 19th centuries give Miller & Arney Antiques a museum gallery air. Oriental porcelain adds splashes of color. ⊠ *1737 Wisconsin Ave. NW,* ☎ *202/338–2369. Metro: Foggy Bottom.*

Old Print Gallery. The capital's largest collection of old prints and maps (including Washingtoniana) is housed in this gallery. ⊠ *1220 31st St. NW,* ☎ *202/965–1818. Metro: Foggy Bottom.*

Retrospective. A small shop crammed with high-quality furniture and accessories, mostly from the '40s and '50s, Retrospective is a place where you can still buy the princess phone that lit up your nightstand in 1962 and the plates your mother served her meat loaf on. ⊠ *2324 18th St. NW,* ☎ *202/483–8112. Metro: Dupont Circle.*

Susquehanna. The largest antiques shop in Georgetown, Susquehanna specializes in American furniture and paintings. ⊠ *3216 O St. NW,* ☎ *202/333–1511. Metro: Foggy Bottom.*

Uniform. The best of the vintage clothing and household accessories shops in the Adams-Morgan neighborhood, Uniform has a vast assortment from the '50s and '60s: piles of fatigue, Nehru, and tie-died shirts, Sergeant Pepper jackets, navy pea coats, and all sorts of other formerly ordinary stuff now prized as icons of a bygone era. You'll also find lava lamps, pillbox hats, feathered mules, Lucite heels, and plateware that could have been props for the Jetsons. ⊠ *2407 18th St. NW,* ☎ *202/483–4577. Metro: Woodley Park.*

Books
Chapters. A "literary bookstore," Chapters eschews cartoon collections and diet guides, filling its shelves instead with serious contemporary fiction, classics, and poetry. ⊠ *1512 K St. NW,* ☎ *202/347–5495. Metro: McPherson Square.*

Cheshire Cat. This bookstore for children carries records, cassettes, posters, and books on parenting. It's a 15-minute walk from the nearest Metro. ⊠ *5512 Connecticut Ave. NW,* ☎ *202/244–3956. Metro: Friendship Heights.*

Kramerbooks. Open 24 hours on weekends, Kramerbooks shares space with a café that has late-night dining and weekend entertainment. The stock is small but well selected. ⊠ *1517 Connecticut Ave. NW,* ☎ *202/387–1400. Metro: Dupont Circle.*

Lammas Books. A selection of music by women as well as women's and lesbian literature is for sale here. ⊠ *1426 21st St. NW,* ☎ *202/775–8218. Metro: Dupont Circle.*

Second Story Books. A mecca for bibliophiles that encourages hours of browsing, this used-books and records emporium is on Dupont Circle. ⊠ *2000 P St. NW,* ☎ *202/ 659–8884. Metro: Dupont Circle.*

Trover Books. The latest political volumes and out-of-town newspapers are here. ⊠ *221 Pennsylvania Ave. SE,* ☎ *202/ 547–2665. Metro: Union Station.*

Children's Clothing and Toys

F.A.O. Schwarz. The most upscale of toy stores, F.A.O. Schwarz carries such items as a toy car (a Mercedes, of course) that costs almost as much as the real thing. Among the other imports are stuffed animals (many larger than life), dolls, and children's perfumes. ⊠ *Georgetown Park, 3222 M St. NW,* ☎ *202/342–2285. Metro: Foggy Bottom.*

Kid's Closet. The downtown choice for baby clothes and shower gifts, The Kid's Closet also stocks some togs for older children. ⊠ *1226 Connecticut Ave. NW,* ☎ *202/429– 9247. Metro: Dupont Circle.*

Crafts and Gifts

American Hand. This is a wonderful place for one-of-a-kind functional and nonfunctional pieces by America's foremost ceramic artists. Georgetown's American Hand also carries limited edition objects for home and office, such as architect-designed dinnerware. ⊠ *2906 M St. NW,* ☎ *202/ 965–3273. Metro: Foggy Bottom.*

Appalachian Spring. Appalachian Spring's two Washington stores sell traditional and contemporary crafts, including quilts, jewelry, weavings, pottery, and blown glass. ⊠ *1415 Wisconsin Ave. NW,* ☎ *202/337–5780;* ⊠ *Union Station,* ☎ *202/682–0505. Metro: Union Station.*

Indian Craft Shop. Handicrafts, including jewelry, pottery, sand paintings, weavings, and baskets from almost two dozen Native American tribes—including Navajo, Pueblo, Zuni, Cherokee, Lakota, and Seminole—are for sale. Items range from inexpensive (as little as $6) jewelry on up to collector-quality antiques costing more than $1,000. ⊠ *Dept. of Interior, 1849 C St. NW, Room 1023,* ☎ *202/208–4056. Metro: Farragut West.*

Martin's. Martin's is a long-established Georgetown purveyor of china, crystal, and silver. ⊠ *1304 Wisconsin Ave. NW,* ☎ *202/338–6144.*

Music Box Center. An exquisite specialty store, the Music Box Center provides listening opportunities via more than 1,500 music boxes that play a total of 500 melodies. ⊠ *918 F St. NW,* ☎ *202/783–9399. Metro: Gallery Place.*

Phoenix. The Phoenix sells Mexican crafts, including folk art, silver jewelry, fabrics, and native and contemporary clothing in natural fibers. ⊠ *1514 Wisconsin Ave. NW,* ☎ *202/338–4404.*

Skynear and Company. The owners of Skynear and Company travel the world to find the unusual: an extravagant assortment of rich textiles, furniture, and home accessories for the art of living. ⊠ *2122 18th St. NW,* ☎ *202/797–7160. Metro: Dupont Circle;* ⊠ *Mazza Gallerie, 5300 Wisconsin Ave. NW,* ☎ *202/362–7541. Metro: Friendship Heights.*

Jewelry
Charles Schwartz & Son. A full-service jeweler, Charles Schwartz specializes in precious stones in traditional and modern settings. Fine watches are also offered. ⊠ *Mazza Gallerie, 5300 Wisconsin Ave. NW,* ☎ *202/363–5432. Metro: Friendship Heights.*

Pampillonia Jewelers. Traditional designs in 18-karat gold and platinum are found here, including many pieces for men. ⊠ *Mazza Gallerie,* ☎ *202/363–6305. Metro: Friendship Heights;* ⊠ *1213 Connecticut Ave. NW,* ☎ *202/628–6305. Metro: Farragut North.*

Tiny Jewel Box. The Tiny Jewel Box sells well-chosen estate jewelry, contemporary jewelry, and unique gifts. ⊠ *1147 Connecticut Ave. NW,* ☎ *202/393–2747. Metro: Farragut North.*

Men's and Women's Clothing

Britches of Georgetown. Britches carries an extensive selection of traditional but trend-conscious designs in natural fibers for men. ⊠ *1219 Connecticut Ave. NW,* ☎ *202/347–8994. Metro: Farragut North;* ⊠ *1247 Wisconsin Ave. NW,* ☎ *202/338–3330.*

Brooks Brothers. The oldest men's store in America, Brooks Brothers has sold traditional formal and casual clothing since 1818. It is the largest men's specialty store in the area and has a small women's department as well. ⊠ *1840 L St. NW,* ☎ *202/659–4650. Metro: Farragut North;* ⊠ *5504 Wisconsin Ave.,* ☎ *301/654–8202. Metro: Friendship Heights.*

Burberrys. Burberrys made its reputation with the trench coat, but this British company also manufactures traditional men's and women's apparel. ⊠ *1155 Connecticut Ave. NW,* ☎ *202/463–3000. Metro: Farragut North.*

Commander Salamander. This funky outpost selling leather, chains, and silver skulls is as much entertainment as shopping; it's open until 10 on weekends. ⊠ *1420 Wisconsin Ave. NW,* ☎ *202/337–2265. Metro: Foggy Bottom.*

J. Press. J. Press was founded in 1902 as a custom shop for Yale University. It is a resolutely traditional clothier: Shetland wool sport coats are a specialty. ⊠ *1801 L St. NW,* ☎ *202/857–0120. Metro: Farragut North.*

Kobos. A rainbow of clothing and accessories imported from West Africa is for sale at Kobos. ⊠ *2444 18th St. NW,* ☎ *202/332–9580. Metro: Dupont Circle.*

Music

Olsson's Books & Records. Olsson's has a good classical and folk music selection. Hours vary significantly from store to store. ✉ *1239 Wisconsin Ave. NW,* ☎ *202/338–9544. Metro: Foggy Bottom;* ✉ *1307 19th St. NW,* ☎ *202/785– 1133. Metro: Dupont Circle;* ✉ *1200 F St. NW,* ☎ *202/ 347–3686. Metro: Metro Center;* ✉ *418 7th St. NW,* ☎ *202/638–7610. Metro: Gallery Place.*

Orpheus Records. Orpheus Records specializes in new and used jazz, rock, and blues records. ✉ *3249 M St. NW,* ☎ *202/337–7970.*

Serenade Record Shop. This shop is especially strong in classical music. ✉ *1800 M St. NW,* ☎ *202/452–0075. Metro: Farragut North.*

Tower Records. The 16,000-square-ft Tower Records offers Washington's best selection of music in all categories, plus videos and laser discs. ✉ *2000 Pennsylvania Ave. NW,* ☎ *202/331–2400. Metro: Foggy Bottom.*

Shoes

Church's. Church's is an English company whose handmade men's shoes are noted for their comfort and durability. ✉ *1820 L St. NW,* ☎ *202/296–3366. Metro: Farragut North.*

Shoe Scene. The fashionable, moderately priced shoes for women found here are direct imports from Europe. ✉ *1330 Connecticut Ave. NW,* ☎ *202/659–2194. Metro: Farragut North.*

Women's Clothing

Ann Taylor. Ann Taylor sells sophisticated, trend-conscious fashions for women and has an excellent shoe department. ✉ *1720 K St. NW,* ☎ *202/466–3544. Metro: Farragut West;* ✉ *3222 M St. NW,* ☎ *202/338–5290;* ✉ *Mazza Gallerie, 5300 Wisconsin Ave. NW,* ☎ *202/244–1940. Metro: Friendship Heights;* ✉ *Union Station,* ☎ *202/371–8010. Metro: Union Station.*

Betsey Johnson. This shop sells fanciful frocks for the young and restless. ✉ *1319 Wisconsin Ave. NW,* ☎ *202/ 338–4090. Metro: Foggy Bottom;* ✉ *Fashion Centre at Pentagon City, 1100 S. Hayes St., Arlington, VA,* ☎ *703/415– 3571. Metro: Pentagon City.*

Chanel Boutique. The Willard Hotel annex is where to find goodies from this legendary house of fashion. ✉ *1455*

Pennsylvania Ave. NW, ☎ 202/638–5055. Metro: Metro Center.

Rizik Bros. Rizik Bros. is a Washington institution combining designer clothing and accessories with expert service. The sales staff is trained to find just the right style from the large inventory, and prices are right. Take the elevator up from the northwest corner of Connecticut and L streets. ✉ *1100 Connecticut Ave. NW, ☎ 202/223–4050. Metro: Farragut North.*

INDEX

X = *restaurant*, 🏨 = *hotel*

NOTES

NOTES

NOTES

NOTES

NOTES

NOTES

NOTES

NOTES

Fodor's Travel Publications

Available at bookstores everywhere, or call 1–800–533–6478, 24 hours a day.

Gold Guides

U.S.

Alaska	Florida	New Orleans	Seattle & Vancouver
Arizona	Hawai'i	New York City	The South
Boston	Las Vegas, Reno, Tahoe	Pacific North Coast	U.S. & British Virgin Islands
California		Philadelphia & the Pennsylvania Dutch Country	USA
Cape Cod, Martha's Vineyard, Nantucket	Los Angeles		Virginia & Maryland
	Maine, Vermont, New Hampshire	The Rockies	Walt Disney World, Universal Studios and Orlando
The Carolinas & Georgia	Maui & Lāna'i	San Diego	
Chicago	Miami & the Keys	San Francisco	Washington, D.C.
Colorado	New England	Santa Fe, Taos, Albuquerque	

Foreign

Australia	Europe	Mexico	Provence & the Riviera
Austria	Florence, Tuscany & Umbria	Montréal & Québec City	Scandinavia
The Bahamas		Moscow, St. Petersburg, Kiev	Scotland
Belize & Guatemala	France		Singapore
Bermuda	Germany	The Netherlands, Belgium & Luxembourg	South Africa
Canada	Great Britain		South America
Cancún, Cozumel, Yucatán Peninsula	Greece	New Zealand	Southeast Asia
Caribbean	Hong Kong	Norway	Spain
China	India	Nova Scotia, New Brunswick, Prince Edward Island	Sweden
Costa Rica	Ireland		Switzerland
Cuba	Israel	Paris	Thailand
The Czech Republic & Slovakia	Italy	Portugal	Toronto
	Japan		Turkey
Eastern & Central Europe	London		Vienna & the Danube Valley
	Madrid & Barcelona		

Special-Interest Guides

Adventures to Imagine	Great American Learning Vacations	Kodak Guide to Shooting Great Travel Pictures	Walt Disney World for Adults
Alaska Ports of Call			Weekends in New York
Ballpark Vacations	Great American Sports & Adventure Vacations	National Parks and Seashores of the East	
Caribbean Ports of Call		National Parks of the West	Wendy Perrin's Secrets Every Smart Traveler Should Know
The Complete Guide to America's National Parks	Great American Vacations		
	Great American Vacations for Travelers with Disabilities	Nights to Imagine	Where Should We Take the Kids? California
Disney Like a Pro		Rock & Roll Traveler Great Britain and Ireland	
Europe Ports of Call			Where Should We Take the Kids? Northeast
Family Adventures	Halliday's New Orleans Food Explorer	Rock & Roll Traveler USA	
Fodor's Gay Guide to the USA		Sunday in San Francisco	Worldwide Cruises and Ports of Call
Fodor's How to Pack	Healthy Escapes		

Fodor's Special Series

WHEREVER
YOU TRAVEL,
*H*ELP IS NEVER
FAR AWAY.

From planning your trip to providing travel assistance
along the way, American Express® Travel Service Offices
are always there to help you do more.

Washington, D.C.

American Express Travel Service
1150 Connecticut Avenue N.W.
202/457-1300

American Express Travel Service
Mazza Gallerie, 5300 Wisconsin N.W.
202/362-4000

American Express Travel Service
Washington Center
1001 G Street, N.W.
202/393-2368

do more AMERICAN EXPRESS
Travel

http://www.americanexpress.com/travel
**American Express Travel Service Offices
are located throughout the United States.
For the office nearest you, call 1-800-AXP-3429.**